The Dead Sea Scrolls
and Christian Faith

FAITH AND SCHOLARSHIP COLLOQUIES SERIES

What Has Archaeology to Do with Faith?
The Old and New Testaments
Images of Jesus Today
Earthing Christologies
The Dead Sea Scrolls and Christian Faith

The Dead Sea Scrolls and Christian Faith

In Celebration of the Jubilee Year
of the Discovery of Qumran Cave I

Edited by
James H. Charlesworth
and Walter P. Weaver

Faith and Scholarship Colloquies

Trinity Press International   Harrisburg, Pa.

First Published 1998

Trinity Press International, P.O. Box 1321, Harrisburg, PA 17105
Trinity Press International is a division of the Morehouse Group

Copyright © 1998 Trinity Press International

Cover Design by Brian Preuss

Library of Congress Cataloging-in-Publication Data

The Dead Sea scrolls and Christian faith : in celebration of the
   jubilee year of the discovery of Qumran cave 1 / edited by James H.
Charlesworth and Walter P. Weaver.
       p.   cm. – (Faith and scholarship colloquies)
   Includes bibliographical references and index.
   ISBN 1-56338-232-6
   1. Dead Sea scrolls – Relation to the Testament. 2. Christianity –
Origin.   I. Charlesworth, James H.   II. Weaver, Walter P.
III. Series.
BM487.D449   1998
296.1'55–dc21   98-9269
                                                                                    CIP

Printed in the United States of America

98   99   00   01   02   10   9   8   7   6   5   4   3   2   1

Contents

Contributors

JAMES H. CHARLESWORTH is the George W. Collord Professor of New Testament Language and Literature at Princeton Theological Seminary and Director of the Princeton Dead Sea Scrolls Project.

JOHN J. COLLINS is Professor of Hebrew Bible and Post-Biblical Judaism in the Divinity School, University of Chicago.

JOSEPH A. FITZMYER, S.J., is Professor Emeritus of Biblical Studies, Catholic University of America.

DAVID NOEL FREEDMAN is Chair in Hebrew Biblical Studies Emeritus, University of California, San Diego.

WALTER P. WEAVER is Professor of Religion Emeritus, Florida Southern College.

Series Description

Faith and Scholarship Colloquies

This series explores the boundaries where faith and academic study intersect. At these borders, the sharp edge of current biblical scholarship is allowed to cut theologically and pose its often challenging questions for traditional faith. The series includes contributions from leading scholars in contemporary biblical studies. As Christian faith seeks to send a word on target in our day, as powerful as those in the past, it needs to sharpen its perception and proclamation from honest and truthful insights in human knowledge, from first-century archaeology to modern linguistics.

Preface

The Challenge of the Dead Sea Scrolls to Christian Faith

Interest in the Dead Sea Scrolls is unparalleled, and it usually arises from their possible challenge to traditional Christian faith. As the evangelists and Paul stressed, Christian faith is based not on reason but on historical events in ancient Palestine and their meaning for those who believe in Jesus as the Christ or the One who was to come. That exposes the fact that Christians confess that Jesus' crucifixion was not a failure of a mission, but the painful and humiliating obedience of God's Son, and that his resurrection by God vindicated his unique message and relation to God. Thus, documents from Jesus' time may shed so much light on events of his time and on his life that faith may be blinded — or even questioned or put in doubt.

Do the Dead Sea Scrolls hinder or undermine Christian faith? Neither confessional interpretations of Jesus' crucifixion nor belief in his resurrection by God can be disproved by any thought or idea in the Dead Sea Scrolls. They never mention Jesus, and thus cannot falsify what is claimed about him. They also do not name or refer to any of Jesus' followers.

Why, then, are the Dead Sea Scrolls so sensationally significant for a better understanding of Christian origins? How and in what ways do these ancient Jewish scrolls alter or reshape Christians' perceptions of Jesus and his earliest followers? What is the proper method for comparing these scrolls with the writings in the New Testament? How do they help us understand prophecy and messianic beliefs during the time when Jesus taught in Galilee and Judaea?

These questions led the biblical professors at Florida Southern College to organize a symposium on the Dead Sea Scrolls and Christian origins. Joseph A. Fitzmyer, S.J., one of the acknowledged specialists on the scrolls from the 1950s to the present, and the author of both *The Dead Sea Scrolls: Major Publications and Tools for Study* and *Responses to 101 Questions on the Dead Sea Scrolls,* was asked to offer for publication a paper on how to compare the scrolls and the New Testament, which was presented to the Prague meeting of the Studiorum Novi Testamenti Societas. David Noel Freedman, a leading expert on the Dead Sea Scrolls since the 1950s and editor of the Anchor Bible and the *Anchor Bible Dictionary,* was invited to survey the history of prophecy and explain the resurgence of prophecy after the Maccabean revolt, as evidenced in the Dead Sea Scrolls and in the life and teachings of Jesus and his followers. John J. Collins, an authority among the new generation of scroll specialists, editor of the *Journal of Biblical Literature,* and author of *The Scepter and the Star: The Messiahs of the Dead Sea Scrolls and Other Ancient Literature,* was asked to share his expert insights into Qumran messianism and the possible impact of the scrolls upon early "Christian" messianism. I was asked to assess how and in what ways the scrolls challenge and help shape Christian faith.

It will become clear to the reader of these chapters how the Dead Sea Scrolls seem to have revolutionized our understanding of Christian origins. For example, Luke seems to have known the document called *An Aramaic Apocalypse* (4Q246), since he shares with the author of this composition three key and unusual phrases: "he will be great," "he will be called Son of the Most High," and "he will be called Son of God." While the Qumran author seems to attribute these characteristics to the coming Messiah, Luke, probably inheriting the imagery from this document by some yet unperceived means, attributed them to the birth of Jesus. The resurgence of prophecy at Qumran helps us understand the phenomenon of prophetic preaching in Paul's letters and in the early Palestinian Jesus Movement. Prior to the discovery of the Dead Sea Scrolls we scholars had only short, usually uninteresting, inscriptions from Jesus' time, and we had to work from edited medieval copies of most of the writings that we thought might have been written during the crucial period of Christian origins, that is, from the early second century B.C.E. to the middle of the second century C.E. Now, as Fitzmyer states in his essay, the Dead Sea Scrolls supply us with firsthand information about the Palestinian Jewish matrix out of which early Christianity and its canonical writings emerged and developed. In the past decades I have held scrolls composed and read by Jews who lived in Palestine when Jesus began his ministry in Galilee, proclaiming God's good news, and using language that would be familiar to many Essenes, the authors of the Dead Sea Scrolls.

Many of the dreams and concepts at Qumran help us understand Jesus' original message and its enduring challenge for Christians today. I have tried to develop my position and report my research in *Jesus and the Dead Sea Scrolls*. I am convinced that hearing the voices of the authors of the Dead Sea Scrolls, and those of the authors collected in this volume, will help us Christians be more attentive to the way it all began. Surely, that can serve as a cure for some of the errors that have misled many leaders of the institutional church — and not only recently but over almost two thousand years. It is my hope that the research and reflections presented in this volume will lead many to read the Dead Sea Scrolls, reread the New Testament, and reflect on what life was like back then when Jews became excited by such prophetic leaders as the Righteous Teacher of Qumran and the Righteous One behind the Good News.

James H. Charlesworth

Acknowledgments

This work arose out of a continuing series of symposia at Florida Southern College relating to issues in biblical studies. The series has been made possible by the support of the college, the efforts of the Department of Religion and Philosophy, and various other groups and persons. Among these are the president of the college, Dr. Thomas Reuschling; the Lucy Ball DuPont Foundation; and Mrs. Frances DeMott of Winter Haven, Florida, whose generosity has contributed significantly to the establishment of a continuing endowment for these symposia. A special note of thanks goes to the secretary of the department, Mrs. Beverly Johnson, for her continuing competence in assisting with the preparation of the manuscript.

Walter P. Weaver

Abbreviations

1QapGen	*Genesis Apocryphon*
1QM	*Milḥāmāh (War Scroll)*
1QpHab	*Pesher on Habakkuk*
1QS	*Serek hayyaḥad (Rule of the Community, Manual of Discipline)*
1QSa	Appendix A (*Rule of the Congregation*) to 1QS
1QSb	Appendix B (*Blessings*) to 1QS
4Q246	*An Aramaic Apocalypse*
4QFlor	*Florilegium* (or *Eschatological Midrashim*) from Qumran Cave 4
4QMMT	*Miqsat Ma'aseh Torah* from Qumran Cave 4
AASOR	Annual of the American Schools of Oriental Research
AB	Anchor Bible
ABD	*Anchor Bible Dictionary*
ASOR	American Schools of Oriental Research
BA	*Biblical Archaeologist*
BARev	*Biblical Archaeology Review*
BASOR	*Bulletin of the American Schools of Oriental Research*
Bib	*Biblica*

CBQ	*Catholic Biblical Quarterly*
CD	Cairo (Genizah text of the) *Damascus* (*Document*)
DJD	Discoveries in the Judean Desert
ErIsr	Eretz Israel
FilNeotest	Filología Neotestamentica
HeyJ	*Heythrop Journal*
HTR	*Harvard Theological Review*
JBL	*Journal of Biblical Literature*
JJS	*Journal of Jewish Studies*
JNES	*Journal of Near Eastern Studies*
JSP	*Journal for the Study of the Pseudepigrapha*
JSPSup	Journal for the Study of Pseudepigrapha — Supplement Series
JSS	*Journal of Semitic Studies*
JTS	*Journal of Theological Studies*
KlT	Kleine Texte
NovTSup	Novum Testamentum, Supplements
NTS	*New Testament Studies*
NTTS	New Testament Tools and Studies
PEQ	*Palestine Exploration Quarterly*
RB	*Revue biblique*
RevQ	*Revue de Qumran*
SBLMS	SBL Monograph Series
SBLRBS	SBL Resources for Biblical Study
SBT	Studies in Biblical Theology
SJLA	Studies in Judaism in Late Antiquity
SNTSMS	Society for New Testament Studies Monograph Series
SPB	Studia postbiblica
VT	*Vetus Testamentum*

Chapter 1

The Dead Sea Scrolls and Christian Origins: General Methodological Considerations

Joseph A. Fitzmyer, S.J.

The Dead Sea Scrolls have proved to be of immense value in the study of the ancient languages of Judea, especially Aramaic and Hebrew, which were in use in Judea in the first centuries B.C.E. and C.E. The scrolls have also assisted significantly in the study of the history of ancient Judaism in the same period, in the examination of the text of the Old Testament, and above all in the study of the Palestinian Jewish matrix of Christianity. The purpose of this chapter is to consider some methodological issues in using the Dead Sea Scrolls for the study of the Palestinian Jewish matrix.

My comments about methodology will fall into three categories: the different senses of "Dead Sea Scrolls"; the privileged character of this newly acquired literature for New Testament study; and some of the risks that this sort of study runs.

DIFFERENT SENSES OF "DEAD SEA SCROLLS"

At the outset, we have to be clear about what we mean by "Dead Sea Scrolls," since the term is used at times in different ways. In a broad sense, it is used to embrace the scrolls and fragments found at eight or nine different locations. This usage stems in part from the way popularizers and sometimes even scholars refer to such documents. In the list I would have to include the following localities:

1. The eleven Qumran caves
2. Masada
3. The caves of Wadi Murabba'at
4. The caves of Wadi Khabra (Naḥal Ḥever)
5. The cave of Wadi Seiyal (Naḥal Ṣe'elim)
6. The cave of Wadi Mahras (Naḥal Mišmar)
7. Khirbet Mird
8. The Genizah of the Synagogue of Ezra in Old Cairo
9. According to some, even the cave of Wadi ed-Daliyeh (the Samaritan Papyri)

The term "Dead Sea Scrolls" is also used in a narrow sense to denote the scrolls and fragments recovered from eleven caves in the vicinity of Khirbet Qumran, and texts related to them, found either at Masada or in the Cairo Genizah. In the case of the Cairo Genizah, one would have to restrict the discussion to texts recovered there that have some relation to those of Qumran, such as the *Damascus Document* or the *Testament of Levi.*[1] The texts found at Masada include some that are copies of Qumran texts and others that seem to have been copied by the same scribes as some Qumran texts. It may even be that some texts copied at Qumran made their way to Masada, when some of the Qumran Community members joined the Jews who took their last stand at Masada against the Romans in 73 C.E.[2]

Among the documents from other localities mentioned above, some would have only a remote connection with the study of early Christianity.[3] For instance, the letters of Bar Cochba from the time of the Second Revolt of Palestinian Jews against Rome (132–35 C.E.) give us new and important evidence of aspects of that revolt put down by the Romans in the early second Christian century. Those documents also bear witness to the Aramaic, Greek, and Hebrew languages in contemporary usage in Judea of the period concerned.[4]

In this regard, the texts of Wadi ed-Daliyeh, the Samaritan Papyri, may also be of some remote interest. They do come from a postexilic period of Judah and shed light on a little-known time of ancient Jewish history, in alluding to some historical figures[5] and revealing the kind of Aramaic then being used.[6] These scrolls, however, are mostly legal documents, and have little to do with the study of either Qumran literature or early Christianity. One may wonder, then, why they are included, even in the broad sense of the term. The reason is that texts from Wadi ed-Daliyeh are to be published in a coming volume of Discoveries in the Judaean Desert, the same Clarendon Press series in which many of the Qumran texts have been or are to be published in definitive form. They have also been officially listed in the Dead Sea Scroll Inventory.[7]

In a similar way, one might wonder why texts from Khirbet Mird are being included, since most of them date from the fifth to the tenth centuries C.E.[8] In this case, it is because of the association of these documents with the Qumran texts in popular discussions,[9] and because the site was discovered more or less about the time that the first Qumran caves were found. Initially, the texts were thought to be related, but subsequently it was discovered that they are completely unrelated.

The upshot of this discussion is that for the study of early Christianity it is "Dead Sea Scrolls" in the narrow or restricted sense on which we must concentrate, that is, on the texts of Qumran, and some texts from Masada and the Cairo Genizah related to these.

THE PRIVILEGED CHARACTER OF
THIS NEWLY ACQUIRED JUDEAN LITERATURE
FOR NEW TESTAMENT STUDY

If I have restricted "Dead Sea Scrolls" to its narrow sense, still another general methodological consideration has to be made. The Qumran texts, fragmentary though many of them are, supply us with firsthand information about the Palestinian Jewish matrix out of which early Christianity and its canonical writings emerged and developed. Even though most of the Greek writings of the New Testament stem from extra-Palestinian or extra-Judean proveniences, a good number of them manifest their connection with that Palestinian Jewish matrix.[10] The Gospels and Acts depict for us the life and ministry of a first-century Palestinian Jew, Jesus of Nazareth, and the early stages of the first Jewish Christian church in Jerusalem and elsewhere in Palestine, before the Christian message spread "to the end of the earth" (Acts 1:8).

Before the discovery of Qumran Cave 1 in 1947, the amount of firsthand information about Palestinian Judaism was limited indeed. It consisted mostly of sparse inscriptions in Aramaic, Greek, and Hebrew.[11] There was also the information that Flavius Josephus had included in his Greek writings, which, being composed roughly about the same time as many of the New Testament writings, have shed important light on the Palestinian Jewish matrix of early Christianity. Though some have questioned at times Josephus's reliability as a historian, his testimony, coming from a Palestinian Jew, has been without equal.[12] Philo's writings, too, have sometimes been important, but they do not always reflect the desirable Palestinian background, and because they are cast in a philosophical mold and indulge in Alexandrian allegorical interpretation of the Old Testament, they are not so useful for the understanding of early Christianity or the interpretation of the New Testament.[13]

Given this situation, one realizes the overall importance of the Qumran texts as a reflection of Palestinian Judaism imme-

diately prior to and contemporary with the life and ministry of
Jesus of Nazareth and with the emergence of early Christianity and its writings. In general, the Qumran texts date from the
end of the third century B.C.E. to a short time before the destruction of the community center in the summer of 68 C.E. at
what is called today Khirbet Qumran. These dates are derived
from the paleographic studies of various scholars who have de-
voted their time and skill to this endeavor.[14] These paleographic
studies have recently been supported in an unexpected way by
radiocarbon datings. Unfortunately, not all the texts have been
so dated, but the general confirmation that has come for the paleographic dating from the radiocarbon dating is, by and large,
noteworthy.[15] It certainly puts to rest the outlandish claims
made by some students of the Qumran scrolls who questioned
or ignored the paleographic datings.[16]

Such a dating of the Qumran texts gives these documents
a status that is privileged for the study of early Christianity.
But it is also necessary in this regard to make some distinc-
tions, for the Qumran scrolls and fragments fall today into three
generic categories, not all of equal value for the study of the
New Testament. First, there are the "biblical" texts, which are
copies of books of the Old Testament. Though these are precious for the text-critical study of the Hebrew Scriptures, they
bear only indirectly on the study of the New Testament; they
may bear witness to a Hebrew substratum of the Greek Old
Testament, the Septuagint, which was normally the text used
by New Testament writers or closely related to their text.[17]

Second, there are the "sectarian" texts. These scrolls are
Hebrew texts composed by members of the Qumran Community and destined for use by them. This would include such
texts as the *Rule of the Community*, the *Damascus Document*, the
Thanksgiving Hymns, the *War Scroll*, various *Pesharim* (biblical
commentaries), and numerous other fragmentary liturgical or
cultic texts that display the theology and tenets that we have
come to associate with the sect of Jews who formed the Community.[18] Whether any of the Qumran Aramaic texts belong to this

category is at the moment debatable, because so few of them seem to contain any of those tenets. The Aramaic texts seem rather to have been composed elsewhere and been imported for use by members of the Qumran Community, which may have resurrected the use of Hebrew as a sacred language for their normal community language.

Third, there is the so-called intertestamental literature, a (Christian) misnomer. This would include all the extrabiblical and parabiblical Jewish literature that is not clearly sectarian. Possibly one should list here the Qumran texts of *Enoch, Jubilees,* various forerunners of the *Testaments of the Twelve Patriarchs,* and much other sapiential, hymnic, and liturgical literature that have come to light. Again such writings may stem from a larger Jewish environment and may simply have been used by members of the Qumran Community, even though they were not composed by them.

For the study of early Christianity and its New Testament writings, the sectarian texts and the so-called intertestamental texts are clearly of great importance. These texts in particular have supplied the *firsthand* information about a form of Palestinian Judaism of the first centuries B.C.E. and C.E., which was known earlier only from reports of Josephus, Philo, and other writers.[19] Such firsthand information has illumined in an unexpected way part of the Jewish matrix of early Christianity.

Another aspect of these Qumran writings, however, has to be considered. Prior to 1947 and the first discovery of Qumran texts, because of the relative paucity of Palestinian Jewish documentation that might be pertinent (apart from Josephus's writings), interpreters of the New Testament often had recourse to rabbinic literature to explain aspects of the Jewish background of the New Testament. That literature was used, but not always with requisite caution. Unfortunately, in some quarters today its use continues without the recognition that it was not written down until c. 200 C.E. It is treated as though it could shed light on first-century Palestinian Judaism, especially of the period prior to the destruction of Jerusalem in 70 C.E.

On the one hand, examples of halakhic writing, which are related to discussions in the later rabbinic writings, have been recovered in the Qumran texts.[20] Such Qumran halakhic texts now manifest that some issues discussed in the rabbinic writings were already alive in the first century B.C.E. or C.E. These Qumran texts, then, serve as a control for the correct use of certain rabbinic material to explain New Testament writings. Such Qumran halakhic material would, then, join Josephus and Philo, who are also on occasion witnesses to the early existence of legal traditions treated in rabbinic texts.

On the other hand, the Qumran texts have brought to light aspects of Palestinian Judaism that differ at times from the rabbinic material. This difference comes from the kind of Judaism that the Qumran texts represent, namely the Essene, whereas the rabbinic tradition is derived from the Pharisaic. For this reason, the dating of the Qumran material gives to these texts a privileged status that has to be correctly estimated in the study of the Palestinian matrix of early Christianity. Consequently, Qumran literature has to be preferred to the later rabbinic literature.[21]

To cite a few examples of the advantage that the Qumran material has over the later rabbinic material in illustrating New Testament issues, I refer to my own comparative study of the use of isolated Old Testament quotations in Qumran literature and in the New Testament.[22] In many instances in the New Testament an Old Testament text is explicitly quoted and introduced with a formula, using either "to say" or "to write." One finds the same device in Qumran texts, especially in the sectarian writings. One also finds the same in the Mishnah, which was codified under the direction of Rabbi Judah the Prince, c. 200 C.E. Here, too, one finds *'āmar,* "he said," and *kātab,* "he wrote," used in similar fashion.[23] There are, of course, some general parallels, but the difference between the specific Mishnaic and Qumran formulas is striking and more numerous than the parallels. There is not one example involving *'āmar* and *kātab* in the Mishnah that is identical with the Qumran examples, and yet the New Testament formulas are often literal Greek translations of many of the Qumran introductory formulas. In other words, the New Testament introductory formulas reflect the first-century Palestinian Jewish usage, already attested in the earlier or contemporary sectarian Qumran texts, whereas the Mishnaic formulas manifest a rabbinic development beyond that of the first-century Qumran usage,[24] which shows that the Mishnaic material is not really adequate for comparison with the New Testament formulas.

In a similar way, one can point to certain Pauline phrases and terminology that one always suspected of being derived from his Jewish background, but that had no counterparts in the Old Testament or in later rabbinic literature. Yet they have now turned up in a remarkable way in Qumran literature.[25] I cite but two examples. The Pauline *erga nomou,* "works of the law," which has often seemed from the way it is used to be a well-known Jewish formula, is never found in the Old Testament or in later rabbinic literature, but it has now turned up in the Jewish writings of Qumran (4QFlor 1–2 i 7: *ma'ăśê tôrāh* ["works of the law"];[26] 4QMMT epilogue: *miqṣāt ma'ăśê hattôrāh* ["more works of the Torah"]).[27] Similarly, the phrase *dikaiosynē theou,* "the righteousness of God," is preserved in 1QM 4:6 (*ṣedeq 'ēl*) and 1QS 10:25 (*ṣidqat 'ēl*).[28]

Other examples of this sort of Palestinian Jewish background of New Testament expressions could be cited.[29]

SOME RISKS THAT THIS STUDY RUNS

The first risk is the temptation to disregard the related archaeological data, the paleographic and radiocarbon dating of the texts, and the contents of the Qumran literature itself. The archaeological data reveal that the eleven caves of Qumran were related to the community center at what is called today Khirbet Qumran. That center was the desert retreat for Jews who lived there in the last century and a half B.C.E. and the first C.E.[30] The contents of the scrolls of their library, biblical, intertestamental, and sectarian, reveal that they come from people of Judea who were Jews to the hilt. The scrolls were not written by Christians, and they have to be accorded their proper place in Jewish history. Chaim Potok in his foreword to a book by L. H. Schiffman has complained about the popular notion that the scrolls were relevant only to the study of nascent Christianity. Very few conceived of them as a window onto early rabbinic Judaism.[31] In his book, Schiffman has rightly sought to reclaim the genuine Jewish heritage for the Qumran scrolls, and anyone who does not recognize that is making a big mistake. This is the mistake of those who have attempted to interpret the texts as Christian or Jewish Christian.[32] These scrolls fill in details about the history of Palestinian Judaism between Alexander the Great and Rabbi Judah the Prince, the codifier of the Mishnah. Schiffman calls the scrolls "documents of various groups of Second Temple Jews whose writings were assembled by a particular sect inhabiting the Qumran settlement during the Hasmonaean and Herodian periods, about 135 B.C.E.–68 C.E."[33] With such a description no one can cavil; nor can one find fault with much of what Schiffman has written about how the Qumran scrolls fit into the history of Judaism of those periods. But, though the subtitle of his book mentions the background of Christianity and one finds in its index a few references to Christianity and Christians, there is no effort made really to discuss that background. For that one will have to go elsewhere.

Part of the background that has made Schiffman write as he does is the fact that so many of the early publications of the scrolls had been entrusted to Christian scholars: three of the seven major texts of Qumran Cave 1; all the other fragments of Cave 1; vols. 1–7, 9, 12–13 in the Discoveries in the Judaean Desert series; and the Enoch fragments of Cave 4. Such Christian scholars were not always attuned to the later rabbinic literature to make the requisite comparisons. But it must be recalled that a political situation was responsible for much of that. Cave 1 was discovered in what was then the British Mandate of Palestine. That came to an end in May 1948 and shortly thereafter the Arab-Jewish War erupted. The State of Israel was formed, and when a truce was finally negotiated, the so-called West Bank came under the domination of the Hashemite Kingdom of Jordan. When the further caves (2–11) were discovered between 1952 and 1956, the scrolls and fragments were found on the West Bank, and not in Israel. Those fragments were brought to the Palestine Archaeological Museum in East Jerusalem for study, where the great jigsaw puzzle was assembled between 1953 and 1960, from which came ultimately about 820 texts. But it was impossible for any Jew to become a member of the international and interconfessional team that was set up to handle that jigsaw puzzle. No Jew was allowed in East Jerusalem, which was cut off from West Jerusalem and from Israel by a mined no-man's land. That is how the Christian scholars came to dominate the study and publication of the Cave 4 fragments. In addition to the glory this has brought them, they have had to shoulder the responsibility of the incredible delay in publication of this important material.

Now in recent times Jewish scholars, among them Schiffman himself, have been brought into the study and publication of the scrolls. Now one can finally get the necessary directives for the proper understanding of the relation of the scrolls to rabbinic literature of the third and later centuries C.E. One must not, however, think that the scrolls are part of rabbinic literature. There is no rabbinic literature that comes to us from the last pre-Christian century or from the first two Christian centuries, or that is needed for the proper understanding of the scrolls of this period of Judaism. Moreover, the Qumran scrolls represent a form of Judaism different from that of the rabbinic tradition, a difference that must be respected.

Even when full recognition is given to the scrolls as Jewish writings, however, there is still plenty of room for the pertinence that they have to nascent Christianity. That is an aspect of the discovery of these scrolls that cannot be denied either. Hence one has to avoid the risk of neglecting the wholly Jewish nature of the scrolls, but also that of neglecting the pertinence of them to nascent Christianity. For they provide new light on the Judean matrix of the New Testament, a light that was not available before 1947.

Another risk is that being run by N. Golb of the University of Chicago, who denies the identification of Khirbet Qumran with any Jewish community center (let alone an Essene one) and believes that it is rather the remains of a (Herodian) fort. He further maintains that the scrolls and fragments found in the various Qumran caves were actually deposits of books brought from various libraries in Jerusalem, possibly even from the Temple itself.[34] He even claims that his interpretation of the scrolls depends on evidence from the so-called *Copper Scroll,* which mentions the hiding of *sĕpārîm,* scrolls or writings.[35]

That some of the scrolls and fragments were copied by Jewish scribes outside of the Qumran scriptorium creates no problem. After all, some of the biblical texts and much of the intertestamental Jewish literature could well have been copied elsewhere and brought to Qumran by Essenes who would have read and studied them there. What was copied at Qumran itself would have been mainly the sectarian literature of the Essenes, even if they did at times also copy other material, biblical or intertestamental. E. Tov believes that he has detected a Qumran system of writing, copying, and orthography.[36] What bearing the Golb thesis would have on the study of early Christianity and of the New Testament might still have to be discussed, if one were to accord it any validity, which I do not.[37]

Still another risk is to fail to recognize the privileged status of the Qumran literature for the study of the New Testament vis-à-vis the rabbinic literature of later date. In this regard, I should have to cite some of the writings of G. Vermes about Jesus of Nazareth.[38] He has often used the Qumran scrolls and fragments in his writings on Jesus, but he has also extrapolated from the rabbinic literature of later centuries in a very questionable fashion.

A different risk comes from the problem created by the

Greek texts of Qumran Cave 7. Scholars are all aware of the attempt by J. O'Callaghan to interpret 7Q4–10 as fragments of New Testament texts.[39] Although most New Testament interpreters have been very reluctant to agree with O'Callaghan, C. P. Thiede has supported him, especially in the identification of 7Q5 as a text of the Gospel of Mark.[40] The Investigations Department (Division of Identification and Forensic Science) of the Israel National Police has photographed the disputed 7Q5 anew and enlarged it, so that it may show that O'Callaghan's reading of line 2 as *autōn* was correct.[41] Moreover, Thiede reports that a computer search has been run at Liverpool, England, on all of Greek literature, classic, hellenistic, and patristic, using the combination of letters as originally proposed by O'Callaghan, and that the only correspondence found for them was Mark 6:52–53. But all of this is highly questionable.[42]

Even if this confirmed reading were to prove acceptable, and if a fragment of Mark were indeed found in Qumran Cave 7, what would that say about all the rest of the fragments of that cave? In itself, the identification of 7Q5 as Marcan may not be impossible, because many scholars have held that the Marcan Gospel was composed c. 65 C.E., that is, a short time prior to the destruction of Jerusalem. If a copy of that Gospel had been brought from Rome or Italy, where many think it was composed, to Christians in Jerusalem in a year or so thereafter, it could have become the property of Jerusalem Christians, who may have wanted to store it for safekeeping in a cave used by Essene friends, when they realized the coming of the siege of Jerusalem by the Romans.

It is usually thought that the Essene community's center at what we call Khirbet Qumran today was destroyed in the summer of 68 C.E., and one usually judges that the caves would have contained their deposits by that time. That would mean that sometime between 65 and the summer of 68 a copy of the Marcan Gospel came to Cave 7.[43] How did it get there? Was it brought by Jerusalem Christians to their Essene neighbors' cave near Khirbet Qumran? Or was it brought by Essenes from

Jerusalem? Who knows? The problem would become even more acute if one insists on the date of the composition of the Marcan Gospel as 70 C.E. (as many do) or later! One realizes today how hypothetical is this identification of 7Q5.[44]

If one could admit that 7Q5 was indeed a fragment of the Gospel according to Mark, what must be said about 7Q4, which O'Callaghan has identified as 1 Tim. 3:16; 4:1, 3?[45] That a copy of a Pastoral Epistle should be found in a Qumran cave prior to 68 C.E. is a major problem!

What evidence is there that would negate or gainsay a deposit of Christian scrolls in Cave 7 at a period later than 68 C.E.? The *Copper Scroll* is a case in point. It mentions sixty-four hiding places where treasures have been buried and written in a form of Hebrew not the same as that of most of the Qumran Hebrew texts, especially the sectarian writings. The *Copper Scroll* has been dated paleographically by J. T. Milik to c. 100 C.E. So the question has been raised whether it might have been deposited in Cave 3 sometime after 70 C.E. If so, then why could not Christian texts have been deposited in Cave 7 at a later date?

If there is any truth in such a claim, what is one to say about the relation of such Qumran discoveries to early Christianity? These, then, are the risks that one must be aware of in the study of the relation of the Dead Sea Scrolls to early Christianity. All of them affect the methodology with which one must undertake such a study.

NOTES

1. Perhaps one should also include the Cairo Genizah Wisdom text. See K. Berger, *Die Weisheitsschrift aus der Kairoer Geniza: Erstedition, Kommentar und Übersetzung*, Texte und Arbeiten zum neutestamentlichen Zeitalter 1 (Tübingen: Francke, 1989). Cf. K. Berger, "Die Bedeutung der wiederentdeckten Weisheitsschrift aus der Kairoer Geniza für das Neue Testament," *NTS* 36 (1990): 415–30.

2. For the Masada texts, see J. A. Fitzmyer, *The Dead Sea Scrolls:*

Major Publications and Tools for Study, rev. ed., SBLRBS 20 (Atlanta: Scholars Press, 1990), 77–78.

3. For a list of such texts, see ibid., 79–90.

4. See J. A. Fitzmyer, "The Bar Cochba Period," in Fitzmyer, *Essays on the Semitic Background of the New Testament* (London: Chapman, 1971; repr. Missoula, Mont.: Scholars Press, 1974), 305–54; S. Applebaum, "The Second Jewish Revolt (A.D. 131–35)," *PEQ* 116 (1984): 35–41; A. Oppenheimer, "The Bar Kokhba Revolt," *Immanuel* 14 (1982): 58–76.

5. See F. M. Cross, "The Papyri and Their Historical Implications," *Discoveries in the Wâdī ed-Dâliyeh*, ed. P. W. Lapp and N. L. Lapp, AASOR 41 (Cambridge, Mass.: ASOR, 1974), 17–29 (+pls. 59–64); Cross, "Samaria Papyrus 1: An Aramaic Slave Conveyance of 335 B.C.E. Found in the Wâdī ed-Dâliyeh," *Nahman Avigad Volume*, ed. J. Aviram, ErIsr 18 (Jerusalem: Israel Exploration Society, 1985), 7*–17* (+pl. II); Cross, "A Reconstruction of the Judean Restoration," *JBL* 94 (1975): 4–18.

6. See D. Gropp, "The Language of the Samaria Papyri: A Preliminary Study," *Sopher Mahir: Northwest Studies Presented to Stanislav Segert* (=*Maarav* 5–6), ed. E. M. Cook (Winona Lake, Ind.: Eisenbrauns, 1990), 169–87.

7. See S. A. Reed, *Dead Sea Scroll Inventory Project: Lists of Documents, Photographs and Museum Plates: Fascicle 12, Wadi ed Daliyeh* (Claremont, Calif.: Ancient Biblical Manuscript Center, 1991).

8. See Fitzmyer, *Dead Sea Scrolls*, 91.

9. See J. T. Milik, *Ten Years of Discovery in the Wilderness of Judaea*, SBT 26 (London: SCM; Naperville, Ill.: Allenson, 1959), 15, 19, 46, 130, 132, 137, 139; F. M. Cross Jr., *The Ancient Library of Qumran and Modern Biblical Studies* (Garden City, N.Y.: Doubleday, 1958), 2, 21 n. 36.

10. It may be that all 27 books of the New Testament come from localities of the eastern Mediterranean area, but some scholars have toyed with the possibility that at least two of them were composed in Palestine itself, James and 1 Peter. See J. N. Sevenster, *Do You Know Greek? How Much Greek Could the First Jewish Christians Have Known?* NovTSup 19 (Leiden: Brill, 1968), 3–4, 11–13.

11. See J. A. Fitzmyer, "The Languages of Palestine in the First Century A.D.," *CBQ* 32 (1970): 501–31; reprinted in slightly revised form in Fitzmyer, *A Wandering Aramean: Collected Aramaic Essays*, SBLMS 25 (Missoula, Mont.: Scholars Press, 1979), 29–56.

12. For a well-written survey of the relation of Josephus's writings to the study of the New Testament, see S. Mason, *Josephus and the New Testament* (Peabody, Mass.: Hendrickson, 1992).

13. Since Philo predates Josephus, his writings would be a better

reflection of Judaism contemporary with Jesus of Nazareth, but it is not a reflection necessarily of *Palestinian* Judaism.

14. See especially F. M. Cross, "The Development of the Jewish Scripts," in *The Bible and the Ancient Near East: Essays in Honor of William Foxwell Albright*, ed. G. E. Wright, Anchor Books (Garden City, N.Y.: Doubleday, 1965), 170–264; N. Avigad, "The Palaeography of the Dead Sea Scrolls and Related Documents," *Aspects of the Dead Sea Scrolls*, Scripta hierosolymitana 4 (Jerusalem: Magnes, 1958), 56–87; S. A. Birnbaum, "The Dates of the Cave Scrolls," *BASOR* 115 (1949): 20–22; "How Old Are the Cave Manuscripts? A Palaeographical Discussion," *VT* 1 (1951): 91–109; "Notes on the Internal and Archaeological Evidence Concerning the Cave Scrolls," *JBL* 70 (1951): 227–32. Cf. Fitzmyer, *Dead Sea Scrolls*, 152.

15. See G. Bonani et al., "Radiocarbon Dating of the Dead Sea Scrolls," *'Atiqot* 20 (1991): 27–32; Bonani, "Radiocarbon Dating of Fourteen Dead Sea Scrolls," *Radiocarbon* 34/3 (1992): 843–49; A. J. Timothy Lull et al., "Radiocarbon Dating of Scrolls and Linen Fragments from the Judean Desert," *Radiocarbon* 37 (1995): 11–19. Cf. S. Goranson, "Radiocarbon Dating the Dead Sea Scrolls," *BA* 54 (1991): 39–42; H. Shanks, "Carbon-14 Tests Substantiate Scroll Dates," *BARev* 17/6 (1991): 72; Z. J. Kapera, "AMS Carbon-14 Dating of the Scrolls," *Qumran Chronicle* 2/1 (1992): 39–42; G. R. Stone, "C-14 Confirms Dead Sea Scroll Dates," *Buried History* 28/1 (1992): 20–22; Stone, "Setting the Record Straight: A Correction and More on the Dead Sea Scroll Datings," *Buried History* 28/4 (1992): 109–22.

16. E.g., all by B. E. Thiering, *Redating the Teacher of Righteousness*, Australian and New Zealand Studies in Theology and Religion 1 (Sydney: Theological Explorations, 1979), 34–49; *The Gospels and Qumran: A New Hypothesis* (Sydney: Theological Explorations, 1981), 4–8; *The Qumran Origins of the Christian Church* (Sydney: Theological Explorations, 1983), 12–14; *Jesus and the Riddle of the Dead Sea Scrolls: Unlocking the Secrets of His Life Story* (San Francisco: HarperSanFrancisco, 1992), 14–19. Also R. H. Eisenman, *Maccabees, Zadokites, Christians and Qumran: A New Hypothesis of Qumran Origins*, SPB 34 (Leiden: Brill, 1983); Eisenman, *James the Just in the Habakkuk Pesher*, SPB 35 (Leiden: Brill, 1986).

17. An example of how such Qumran biblical texts help in the interpretation of the New Testament may be taken from Acts 7:14, which counts the number of people who went down with Jacob to Egypt as seventy-five persons. The MT speaks rather of seventy persons (Gen. 46:27; cf. Exod. 1:5; Deut. 10:22). But the LXX of the first two of these passages reads seventy-five, as do 4QGen-Exoda 17–18:2; 4QExodb 1:5 (DJD 12, 18, 84). Thus these Qumran Cave 4 texts reveal that there

were indeed in pre-Christian Palestine Hebrew texts of Genesis and Exodus that read the same number as the Greek LXX and that the latter version was not erroneous or tendentious.

18. The text 11QTemple is problematic. Does it represent a sectarian text, as Y. Yadin seemed to think, or a pre-Essene document, as others have maintained?

For me the best identification of the Qumran sect is still the Essene. The attempt of L. H. Schiffman and others to relate the Qumran community to the Sadducees is simply misguided, in my opinion. See my article, "The Qumran Community: Essene or Sadducean?" *HeyJ* 36/4 (1995): 467–76. Cf. T. S. Beall, *Josephus' Description of the Essenes Illustrated by the Dead Sea Scrolls,* SNTSMS 58 (New York: Cambridge University Press, 1988).

19. See G. Vermes and M. D. Goodman, *The Essenes according to the Classical Sources,* Oxford Centre Textbooks 1 (Sheffield: JSOT, 1989); A. Adam, *Antike Berichte über die Essener,* 2nd ed., KIT 182 (New York: de Gruyter, 1972).

20. See L. H. Schiffman, *The Halakhah at Qumran,* SJLA 16 (Leiden: Brill, 1975); L. H. Schiffman, ed., *Archaeology and History in the Dead Sea Scrolls: The New York University Conference in Memory of Yigael Yadin,* JSP-Sup 8 (Sheffield: JSOT, 1990), passim; L. H. Schiffman, "Qumran and Rabbinic Halakhah," and J. M. Baumgarten, "Recent Qumran Discoveries and Halakhah in the Hellenistic-Roman Period," both in *Jewish Civilization in the Hellenistic-Roman Period,* ed. S. Talmon (Philadelphia: Trinity Press International, 1991), 138–46, 147–58.

21. When "later rabbinic literature" is used here, I mean the Mishnah, the Tannaitic Midrashim, and the Palestinian Talmud. The use of most of the other rabbinic literature, e.g., the Babylonian Talmud, the Midrash Rabbah, is even more highly questionable, the former because of its provenience (Babylonia) and normal lack of relevance to Palestine, and the latter because of its date. The same would have to be said of all Amoraic, Geonic, and later Jewish material.

In this connection, one has to ask further to what extent something that appears in this later Jewish literature is a reflection of controversy with Christianity. Simply because it is written in a Semitic language, Aramaic or Hebrew, it does not mean that it reflects a tradition earlier than or prior to the Greek New Testament. Moreover, even in the case of the earliest of the rabbinic writings, the Mishnah and Tannaitic Midrashim, the attribution of sayings to a rabbi who may have lived in the first century C.E. does not necessarily mean that the tradition so ascribed goes back to him. We have at length succeeded in getting at least some Christians to realize that not everything put on the lips of Jesus in the Gospels was necessarily uttered by him in the form preserved. But it is now necessary to get Christian scholars who use Jewish rabbinic material to make similar adjustments in their use of that material.

22. Fitzmyer, "The Use of Explicit Old Testament Quotations in Qumran Literature and in the New Testament," *NTS* 7 (1960–61): 297–333; reproduced in slightly revised form in *Essays on the Semitic Background of the New Testament*, 3–58. Cf. F. L. Horton Jr., "Formulas of Introduction in the Qumran Literature," *RevQ* 7 (1969–71): 505–14.

23. See B. M. Metzger, "The Formulas Introducing Quotations of Scripture in the NT and the Mishnah," *JBL* 70 (1951): 297–307; reproduced in slightly revised form in his *Historical and Literary Studies: Pagan, Jewish, and Christian*, NTTS 8 (Leiden: Brill, 1968), 52–63.

24. See further J. M. Baumgarten, "A 'Scriptural' Citation in 4Q Fragments of the Damascus Document," *JJS* 43 (1992): 95–98; G. Vermes, "Biblical Proof-Texts in Qumran Literature," *JSS* 34 (1989): 493–508; M. Fishbane, *Biblical Interpretation in Ancient Israel* (Oxford: Clarendon, 1985), 213–20.

25. See J. A. Fitzmyer, "Paul's Jewish Background and the Deeds of the Law," in *According to Paul: Studies in the Theology of the Apostle* (Mahwah, N.J.: Paulist Press, 1993), 18–35.

26. See J. M. Allegro, *Qumrân Cave 4: I (4Q158–4Q186)*, DJD 5 (Oxford: Clarendon, 1968), 53 (=4Q174). The attempt of J. Strugnell to read *tôrāh* as *tôdāh* has proved to be mistaken. It was already highly questionable that one should *peut-être* read a *daleth* instead of the *resh* that Allegro had originally proposed. See Strugnell's "Notes en marge du volume V des Discoveries in the Judaean Desert of Jordan," *RevQ* 7 (1969–71): 163–276, esp. 221.

27. See E. Qimron and J. Strugnell, *Qumran Cave 4: V. Miqṣat Maʿaśe ha-Torah*, DJD 10 (Oxford: Clarendon, 1994), 62 (C 27; pl. VIII). Cf. their articles, "An Unpublished Halakhic Letter from Qumran," *Biblical Archaeology Today: Proceedings of the International Congress on Biblical Archaeology, Jerusalem April 1984* (Jerusalem: Israel Exploration Society, 1985), 400–407, 429–31; (an abridgement of the preceding article with the same title) *Israel Museum Journal* 4 (1985): 9–12 (with a photo of a fragment containing a column and a half of eight lines of text, in which the phrase is found).

28. In the Old Testament Yahweh is, indeed, said to be *ṣaddîq* (righteous), and there is mention of his *ṣedeq* (righteousness), but the verbatim equivalent of the Pauline phrase is not found. In Deut. 33:21 one does find *ṣidqat Yhwh*, but that is not rendered in Greek as *dikaiosynē theou*; the LXX actually has translated it *dikaiosynēn Kyrios epoiēsen*. Cf. my commentary, *Romans*, AB 33 (New York: Doubleday, 1993), 257–63.

29. For an early survey and discussion of such material, see H. Braun, *Qumran und das Neue Testament*, 2 vols. (Tübingen: Mohr [Siebeck], 1966). Cf. J. Murphy-O'Connor and J. H. Charlesworth, eds., *Paul and the Dead Sea Scrolls* (New York: Crossroad, 1990); J. H. Charlesworth, ed., *John and the Dead Sea Scrolls* (New York: Crossroad, 1990).

30. See R. de Vaux, *Archaeology and the Dead Sea Scrolls*, Schweich Lectures of the British Academy 1959 (London: Oxford University, 1973). This is unfortunately only a preliminary report, and de Vaux died before he could publish the definitive report. It is now being published; see J.-B. Humbert and A. Chambon, *Fouilles de Khirbet Qumran et de Ain Feshkha*, Novum Testamentum et Orbis Antiquus, series archaeologica 1/1 (Fribourg: Editions Universitaires; Göttingen: Vandenhoeck and Ruprecht, 1994), with further parts still to come. Cf. E.-M. Laperrousaz, *Qoumrân: L'Etablissement essénien des bords de la Mer Morte: Histoire et archéologie du site* (Paris: Picard, 1976).

31. Schiffman, *Reclaiming the Dead Sea Scrolls: The History of Judaism, the Background of Christianity, the Lost Library of Qumran* (Philadelphia: Jewish Publication Society, 1994), xi.

32. See n. 16 above.

33. Schiffman, *Reclaiming the Dead Sea Scrolls*, xiii.

34. See N. Golb, *Who Wrote the Dead Sea Scrolls? The Search for the Secret of Qumran* (New York: Scribner's, 1995). Cf. his articles: "Dead Sea Scrolls: A New Perspective," *American Scholar* 58 (1989): 177–207; "Khirbet Qumran and the Manuscripts of the Judaean Wilderness: Observations on the Logic of Their Investigation," *JNES* 49 (1990): 103–14; "The Freeing of the Scrolls and Its Aftermath," *Qumran Chronicle* 2/1 (1992): 3–25; "The Qumran-Essene Hypothesis: A Fiction of Scholarship," *Christian Century* 109 (1992): 1138–43; "The Major Anomalies in the Qumran-Sectarian Theory and Their Resolution," *Qumran Chronicle* 2/3 (1993): 161–82.

35. See 3Q15 8:3. Cf. M. Baillet, J. T. Milik, and R. de Vaux, *Les 'Petites Grottes' de Qumrân*, DJD 3 (Oxford: Clarendon, 1962), 292.

36. See E. Tov, "Hebrew Biblical Manuscripts from the Judaean Desert: Their Contribution to Textual Criticism," *JJS* 39 (1988): 5–37; repr. in slightly revised form in *Jewish Civilization in the Hellenistic-Roman Period*, ed. Talmon, 107–37.

37. See my dissent in "Scroll Origins: An Exchange on the Qumran Hypothesis," *Christian Century* 110/10 (March 24–31, 1993): 326–29.

38. See his *Jesus the Jew: A Historian's Reading of the Gospels* (London: Collins, 1973); *Jesus and the World of Judaism* (London: SCM, 1983); and especially "Jewish Studies and New Testament Interpretation," *JJS* 31 (1980): 1–17. Cf. J. A. Fitzmyer, "Problems of the Semitic Back-

ground of the New Testament," in *The Yahweh/Baal Confrontation and Other Studies in Biblical Literature and Archaeology: Essays in Honour of Emmett Willard Hamrick*, ed. J. M. O'Brien and F. L. Horton Jr., Studies in the Bible and Early Christianity 35 (Lewiston, N.Y.: Mellen Biblical Press, 1995), 80–93.

39. Beginning with "¿Papiros neotestamentarios en la cueva 7 de Qumran?" *Bib* 53 (1972): 91–100. Cf. Fitzmyer, *Dead Sea Scrolls*, 168–722.

40. *The Earliest Gospel Manuscript? The Qumran Papyrus 7Q5 and Its Significance for New Testament Studies* (Carlisle, Cumbria: Paternoster, 1992); "7Q — Eine Rückkehr zu den neutestamentlichen Papyrusfragmenten in der siebten Höhle von Qumran," *Bib* 65 (1984): 538–59; "Neutestamentliche Papyrologie: Die ersten Handschriften, ihre Datierung und Bewertung," *IBW-Journal* 23/10 (1985): 12–19.

41. See C. P. Thiede, "Bericht über die kriminaltechnische Untersuchung des Fragments 7Q5 in Jerusalem," in *Christen und Christliches in Qumran?*, ed. B. Mayer, Eichstätter Studien n.s. 32 (Regensburg: Pustet, 1992), 239–45, esp. 243.

42. Ibid., 240. O'Callaghan's reading of 7Q5 and his claims, even after the rephotographing of the fragment, have recently been subjected to serious criticism. See E. Puech, "Des fragments grecs de la grotte 7 et le Nouveau Testament? 7Q4 et 7Q5 et le Papyrus Magdalen grec 17 = P64," *RB* 102 (1995): 570–84; M.-E. Boismard, "A propos de 7Q5 et Mc 6, 52–53," *RB* 102 (1995): 585–88; P. Grelot, "Note sure les propositions du Pr Carsten Thiede," *RB* 102 (1995): 589–91. [Ed. note: 7Q5 has been identified with other texts: P. Garnet, in *Evangelical Quarterly* 45 (1973): 8–9, claimed it was of Exod. 36:10–11, C. H. Roberts in *JTS* 23 (1972): 446, suggested it is of 2 Kings 5:13–14. J.H.C.]

43. It should be recalled that Cave 7 was hollowed out in antiquity in the southern edge of the plateau on which the community center was located. Unfortunately, even more of it has crumbled into the wadi below since its discovery in 1952, and today one can only see where the cave once was. So little remains of that area that all recent calls for a fresh reexamination of the cave or further excavation of it seem doomed to failure. I visited the site in June 1993.

44. See further the latest claims of J. O'Callaghan, since the Israeli rephotographing of the fragment: "Sobre el papiro de Marcos en Qumran," *FilNeotest* 5 (1992): 191–97; "L'ipotetico papiro di Marco a Qumrân," *Civiltà Cattolica* 143/2 (1992): 464–73.

45. See Thiede, "Bericht," 241 (an enlarged photograph of the fragment). [Ed. note: 7Q4 has been identified with Num. 14:23–24 by G. D. Fee in *JBL* 92 (1973): 109–12, and with *1 Enoch* 103:3–4 by G.-W. Nebe in *RevQ* 13 (1988): 629–32. J.H.C.]

Chapter 2

Ideas of Messianism
in the Dead Sea Scrolls

John J. Collins

The Dead Sea Scrolls are of exceptional importance
for the history of Judaism and Christianity. They come from the
period when the younger religion emerged from the older; and
they now constitute the main corpus of Hebrew and Aramaic
literature from this period. The scrolls have shed light on many
aspects of Judaism from around the turn of the era, but perhaps
the area of greatest importance for Jewish-Christian relations
is that of messianic expectation, since it was the acceptance of
Jesus of Nazareth as the Messiah that initially distinguished his
followers from the rest of Judaism.[1] It would be misleading to
say that messianic expectation plays a central part in the scrolls.
In fact the number of messianic texts is quite modest. Nonetheless, the scrolls throw some new and interesting light on this
aspect of Judaism around the turn of the era.

It may be well to begin with a few general comments on
the nature and provenience of the Dead Sea Scrolls. The first
batch of scrolls discovered, fifty years ago, included a document
known as the *Manual of Discipline,* or the *Rule of the Commu-*

nity. This document set out the regulations for a quasimonastic community, separate from the rest of Judaism, with its own rite of admission and provisions for expulsion. Scholars quickly inferred that this Community had occupied the site of Qumran, adjacent to the caves where the scrolls were found.[2] The Community was further identified as a settlement of the Essene sect, known only from descriptions in Greek and Latin authors, principally Josephus and Philo.[3] The identification was based on two factors. First, Pliny, a Roman author who perished in the eruption of Vesuvius in 79 C.E., wrote that there was an Essene settlement by the Dead Sea, between Jericho and Ein Gedi. No other plausible site for that settlement is known. Second, there are extensive similarities between the description of the Essenes in Josephus and the *Rule of the Community* from Qumran, especially in the complex procedures for admission to the Community.[4]

There are also some noteworthy differences. The Essenes supposedly practiced celibacy, although Josephus notes that this was not true of all Essenes and that one order of the sect married.[5] The scrolls never prescribe celibacy, although they are much concerned with purity and have a restrictive attitude toward sex at several points.[6] The scrolls attest to a whole range of beliefs that are not included in the descriptions of the Essenes, including the expectation of messianic figures and of a final war between "the Sons of Light" and "the Sons of Darkness." Most scholars have held that the similarities outweigh the differences, especially if we bear in mind that the Greek accounts were written by outsiders, whose understanding of the sect may have been deficient. Not all the scrolls found at Qumran were produced by the Essene Community. Some of them, including biblical texts, are clearly older than the Qumran settlement, which dates from the late second century B.C.E. The consensus, however, holds that the scrolls are an Essene library, containing a core of sectarian documents but also some of the literature common to other Jews of the time.

The consensus that the scrolls constitute an Essene library has come under criticism from many quarters in recent years, not least from my colleague at the University of Chicago, Norman Golb.[7] The critics have scored some valid points. Fragments of over eight hundred scrolls have been found in the caves. It is unlikely that they were all copied by the small community at Qumran. (The table that archaeologists had thought was part of a scriptorium may have been a dining table.)[8] Nonetheless, the Essene hypothesis still commands the balance of probability. There are really three issues involved.

First, are the scrolls a sectarian collection, as distinct from being a random sampling of the Judaism of the time or the library? This question, in my judgment, must be answered in the affirmative. There are twelve copies of the *Rule of the Community,* a fact that shows that it was a document of importance. There are also nine copies of another, related, sectarian rule known as the *Damascus Document* and six copies of a letter explaining the legal issues that led the author and his group to break off from the rest of Judaism (4QMMT). Moreover, there is a network of overlapping terminology and allusions between several scrolls, which shows that they are interrelated. We will see an example of this in the case of messianism, but other examples can be given from legal rulings and community organization. It is also noteworthy that no copies of the Maccabean books have been found, although 1 Maccabees was almost certainly written in Hebrew, and there are no examples of identifiably Pharisaic halakah. All these factors argue strongly that *the scrolls are a sectarian collection,* although they may include some writings that circulated more widely.

Second, can the sect be identified as the Essenes? The evidence here is less decisive, but still strong. The similarities in the process of admission are remarkable, and Qumran is right in the area where there was supposed to be an Essene settlement. If the scrolls are Essene, however, then the descriptions of the Essenes by Josephus and Philo are deficient at some points. The alternative is to suppose that there was another sect, very similar to the Essenes in some respects, which was unknown before the discovery of the scrolls. I think it is simpler to suppose that *the sect was in fact Essene.*

Third, did the Community live at the site of Qumran? In view of the proximity to the caves, and the discovery of a cemetery with over one thousand graves, this seems an obvious hypothesis. It has been questioned, however, by scholars who suggest that the site was a military fort[9] or even that it was a private villa.[10] While I think the view that Qumran was a sectarian settlement is overwhelmingly probable, this issue does not make much difference to the discussion of the scrolls. The most important issue is whether the collection is sectarian. If it is, as I contend, then we cannot assume that everything found in the scrolls was representative of Judaism at large, and we must try to distinguish what was commonly held and what was distinctive to the Dead Sea sect at Qumran.

THE DUAL MESSIAHSHIP

Turning now to the subject of messianism, we find a distinctively sectarian idea already in the *Rule of the Community.* There we find that members are to follow the original precepts of the Community "until there shall come the Prophet and the Messiahs of Aaron and Israel."[11] The striking thing about this formulation, of course, is that it predicts not one messiah, but two. Such an idea is rare in Jewish sources, but not unique.[12] The *Damascus Document,* which was found in the Cairo Genizah at the turn of the century, contains a number of references to "the messiah of Aaron and Israel."[13] This phrase could refer to two messiahs rather than one.[14] Several copies of the *Damascus Document* were found at Qumran, and so the use of the plural in the *Rule of the Community* was taken to clarify the meaning here, too. Other parallels between the two documents show that the *Rule of the Community* and the *Damascus Document* are related, and most probably come from the same sect. The notion of a priestly messiah beside the Davidic, royal messiah, has a precedent in the prophet Zechariah, who spoke of "two sons of oil" (Zech. 4:12–14; cf. Zech. 6:11–12). Throughout much of the Second Temple period, before the rise of the Hasmoneans, the high priest was the de facto ruler in Jerusalem. The references in the scrolls anticipate that the high priest would continue to have a dominant role in the end-time. The *Rule of the Community* and the *Damascus Document* both emphasize the authority of "the sons of Zadok, the priests" in the sectarian community, and so it is not surprising that they should also look for a priestly messiah.

The phrase "messiah" or "messiahs of Aaron and Israel" occurs only in the two rulebooks, the *Rule of the Community* and the *Damascus Document*,[15] but the idea of dual messiahship is deeply rooted in the sectarian scrolls. At this point, it may be well to pause and consider what is meant by the word "messiah." The word, of course, means simply "anointed," and can be used with reference to the past as well as to the future. The word is used in the plural a number of times in the scrolls, with reference to the Prophets.[16] In an eschatological context, however, the word acquired a more technical sense. The classic usage, which continued long in Jewish tradition, refers to the King Messiah, the figure who would restore the Davidic kingship.[17] The "messiah of Israel" in the scrolls is presumably this figure, the king of the end-time. A priestly messiah is the high priest of the end-time. Most Jewish texts that speak of the messianic age pay no attention to such a figure. What is distinctive in the Dead Sea Scrolls is the prominence given to the high priest of the end-time. To say that he is a "messiah" implies that he is comparable in rank to the King Messiah. In fact he appears to take precedence over the Messiah of Israel in some cases.

One such case is found in a document called the *Rule of the Congregation* (1QSa), which was probably copied at the end of the *Rule of the Community* on a scroll from Cave 1.[18] The text is fragmentary and some important words are missing. It is introduced as "the rule for all [in] the Congregation of Israel in the end of days." The second column refers to a figure who "shall enter [at] the head of all the Congregation of Israel with all [his] br[others, the Sons of] Aaron, the priests, [who are invited to] the feast, the men of the name. And they shall sit be[fore him, each man] according to his glory. And after [them] the [Messi]ah of Israel [shall enter]. And the heads of the [thousands of Israel] shall sit before him [each m]an according to his glory."[19] The passage goes on to describe how the priest will first bless the bread and wine, and then "the Messiah of Israel" will stretch out "his hand to the bread." The priest evidently takes precedence over the Messiah of Israel. Although he is not called "messiah" in the *Rule of the Congregation*, it seems reasonable to refer to such a figure as a priestly messiah.[20]

The distinctive point about the messianic expectation of the scrolls is that the authority of the King Messiah is qualified and subordinated to that of the priests. A fragmentary commentary on Isaiah expounds the famous passage in Isaiah 11: "There shall come forth a shoot from the stump of Jesse...." The passage is interpreted with reference to the Branch of David, but the commentary continues: "And as for that which He said, *He shall not [judge by what his eyes see] or pass sentence by what his ears hear,* interpreted this means.... As they teach him, so will he judge; and as they order, [so will he pass sentence]. One of the Priests of renown will go out...."[21] In the Bible, the point is that he will be guided by the spirit of the Lord. In the scroll, he will be guided by the instruction of a priest. The Temple Scroll, which is often taken to be a law for the end-time,[22] also provides that when the king sits on the throne of his kingdom, "they shall write for him this law from the book which is before the priests."[23] This provision, of course, is derived from Deut. 17:18: "he shall have a copy of this law, written in the presence of the levitical priests." For the Dead Sea sect the restriction placed on the historical king would also apply to the King Messiah at the end of days.

THE KING MESSIAH

The *Rule of the Community* and the *Damascus Document* say little about the Messiah of Israel except that he is expected to come. A number of other passages are more forthcoming. The commentary on Isaiah alludes to a war with the Kittim, a code word for the Romans which is also used in the *War Scroll*. It also refers to a figure called "the prince of the congregation." It is clear from a number of passages that this "prince" is none other than the King Messiah. The *Blessings* (1QSb), which originally followed the *Rule of the Congregation* at the end of the copy of the *Rule of the Community* from Cave 1, contains a blessing for this prince: "The Master" shall "bless the Prince of the Congregation... and the covenant of the Community he [God] shall renew for himself, [so as] to raise up the kingdom of his people for eve[r...] [and to] reprove with fair[ness the h]umble of the [l]and, and to walk before him perfectly in all the way[s of God] and to raise up a covenan[t...a re]fuge for those who seek hi[m...]."[24] The passage goes on to pray "[May] the Lord [raise you] to eternal heights, and...with your sceptre may you devastate [the] land, and by the breath of your lips may you kill the wicked [ones...]."[25] The language of this blessing is obviously and heavily indebted to Isaiah 11, one of the classic messianic passages in the Hebrew Bible. The Prince is also related to another classic biblical text in the *Damascus Document*. In this case the text is Balaam's oracle in Numbers 24: "The star is the Interpreter of the Law who shall come to Damascus; as it is written, A star shall come forth out of Jacob and a sceptre shall arise out of Israel. The sceptre is the prince of the congregation, and when he comes he shall smite all the children of Sheth." The messianic interpretation of Balaam's oracle was widespread in early Judaism.[26] It is reflected in Philo of Alexandria, a philosophical Jew of the Diaspora with little interest in eschatological matters.[27] It is from this biblical passage that Bar Cochba, "Son of the Star," took (or was given) his name.[28] It was commonly taken to refer to a warrior messiah who would restore the kingdom of Israel.

The expression "Prince of the Congregation" has its background in the priestly writings of the Pentateuch, in which it refers to the leaders of the tribes. The use with reference to a future figure derives from Ezekiel, who uses the term *nasî* for the Davidic ruler: "and I the Lord will be their God, and my servant David shall be prince among them. In the postbiblical period, however, "Prince of the Congregation" is not found as a messianic title outside of the scrolls. (Bar Cochba, however, is called the Prince of Israel.)[29] In the scrolls, the congregation in question is no longer the historical Israel, but the Congregation of the new covenant, or the Congregation of the end of days. It appears, then, to have become a distinctively sectarian title for the Davidic messiah.

Apart from the designation "Prince of the Congregation" and the subjection to priestly authority, however, the portrayal of the King Messiah in these texts corresponds well with what we know of other strands of Judaism at the time. The scrolls also refer to him in other ways: he is the Branch of David,[30] or "the righteous Messiah."[31] Expectation of a Davidic messiah is widely attested around the turn of the era. It is found in such diverse sources as Philo, the Psalms of Solomon, and the Eighteen Benedictions, as well as the scrolls.[32] It is repeatedly linked to a few biblical texts, chiefly Isaiah 11 and Numbers 24, with occasional use of such passages as Genesis 49 and 2 Samuel 7, and the expression "Branch of David" from Jeremiah. The same biblical texts appear with messianic connotations in the Targumim and rabbinic writings of a later period.[33] Consistently in these texts the Messiah is a warrior king, characterized by justice, who will restore the kingdom of Israel.

Thus far I have summarized the messianic expectations of the scrolls which have been well known for several years. Several new texts have recently become available, and these too contain some messianic passages. There are three such texts that I want to consider here: *First*, 4Q285, a fragment of the *War*

Rule, popularly though inaccurately known as "the dying messiah text"; *second,* 4Q246, the so-called *Aramaic Apocalypse,* better known as the "Son of God" text; and *third,* 4Q521, sometimes called *On Resurrection,* which refers to a messiah whom heaven and earth will obey.

A DYING MESSIAH? (4Q285)

4Q285 is a very fragmentary text, consisting of some sixteen fragments, reduced to ten by joining. Controversy has centered on fragment 5, which has six lines, none of them complete.[34] The first line preserves a clear mention of "Isaiah the prophet." Line 2 cites Isa. 11:1: "there shall come forth a shoot from the stump of Jesse." Line 3 mentions "the Branch of David, and they will enter into judgment with...." The fourth line is the controversial one. Wise and Eisenman translate as follows: "they will put to death the Leader of the Community, the Bran[ch of David]."[35] Geza Vermes, and other scholars, have read it as "the Prince of the Congregation, the Branch of David, will kill him."[36] Line 5 contains a reference to wounds, and says that a priest "will command...." The final line of the fragment mentions the Kittim, a familiar designation of the Romans in the *War Scroll* and the Pesharim.

The controversy has raged as to whether this fragment refers to the death of a messiah, an idea which has no clear parallel in Judaism before the rise of Christianity.[37] The interpretation of Wise and Eisenman, that this is a "dying messiah," was publicized widely in the newspapers, presumably on the assumption that it has a bearing on the uniqueness of Christianity.[38] The significance of the controversy can be questioned. Other people who claimed to be messiahs, besides Jesus of Nazareth, were put to death in the first century.[39] Nonetheless it must be said that the messianic pretenders killed by the Romans in the first century were no longer regarded as messiahs after their deaths (except for Jesus of Nazareth). The notion of a messiah ben Joseph, who would be killed in battle, is only attested after the abortive messianic reign of Bar Cochba in the second century C.E.[40]

The more basic question, however, is whether 4Q285 actually refers to a dying messiah. Some have questioned whether it refers to a messiah at all, since the word "messiah" is not mentioned.[41] The clear reference to the Prince of the Congregation and the Branch of David, however, coupled with the citation of Isaiah 11, make clear that a messiah is indeed involved. Line 4 of the fragment, in itself, is ambiguous. If Wise's translation, "they killed the prince of the congregation..." were correct, we should normally expect an object marker before the noun, but this objection is not decisive. The word order might be taken to favor Wise's translation, but again, not decisively. What is decisive is the context. Isaiah 11 speaks clearly of a figure who will kill the wicked with the breath of his lips. It provides no basis for inferring a messiah who would be slain. While biblical texts are sometimes interpreted in surprising ways in the scrolls, such a reversal of the plain sense of the text would be extraordinary. We have seen that the Prince of the Congregation is elsewhere depicted as a victorious warrior, in accordance with the biblical prophecy. There is no parallel for relating the death of either the Prince or the shoot of David to Isaiah 11. In view of this situation, it is overwhelmingly probable that the Messiah also does the killing in 4Q285. The fragment is especially reminiscent of the commentary on Isaiah, with which it shares the detail that "a priest will command" even in the presence of the Messiah.

J. T. Milik has suggested that this fragment is part of the Rule for the eschatological war, which is described most fully in the *War Scroll*.[42] Many scholars have denied that the Messiah has any role in that war.[43] The denial, however, cannot be maintained. The title "Prince of the Congregation" appears in column 5 of the *War Scroll*, where it is written on his shield as part of the preparation for battle. Balaam's oracle about the Star and the Sceptre is also cited without interpretation in col-

umn 11 of the *War Scroll*. In view of these references, and the
fact that the Messiah/Prince of the Congregation clearly has a
role in the eschatological war in the commentary on Isaiah and
in 4Q285, we should surely conclude that he also had a role in
the *War Rule*. The scrolls seem to be quite consistent in giving
the Davidic Messiah an active role in the eschatological conflict.

THE "SON OF GOD" TEXT
(=AN ARAMAIC APOCALYPSE, 4Q246)

The "Son of God" text has been the subject of controversy for
twenty years. In 1972, J. T. Milik presented it in a public lecture
at Harvard, and promised to publish it in the *Harvard Theological Review*. The publication did not follow. Joseph Fitzmyer
published part of the text in an article in 1974,[44] and this publication became the basis for a number of other studies.[45] Finally
the full text was published by Emil Puech in *Revue Biblique,* and
again in the official Discoveries in the Judaean Desert series.[46]

The text consists of two columns, of nine lines each. Column 1 is torn vertically so that one third to one half of each
line is missing, but column 2 is substantially intact. Since column 2 ends with an incomplete sentence, it appears that there
was at least a third column.

The fragmentary opening verse says that someone "fell before the throne." The following verses are apparently addressed
to a king, and refer to "your vision." The passage goes on to say
that "affliction will come on earth . . . and great carnage among
the cities." There is mention of kings of Assyria and Egypt. The
second half of line 7 reads " . . . will be great on earth." Then
column 2 continues as follows:

> "Son of God" he shall be called, and "Son of the Most High"
> he shall be named. Like sparks which you saw, so will be their
> kingdom. For years they will rule on earth, and they will tram-
> ple all. People will trample on people, and city on city [There is
> a blank space at this point] until the people of God arises and

all rest from the sword. His kingdom is an everlasting kingdom and all his ways truth. He will judge the earth with truth and all will make peace. The sword will cease from the earth and all cities will pay him homage. The great God will be his strength. He will make war on his behalf, give nations into his hand and cast them all down before him. His dominion is everlasting dominion and all the depths. . . . [47]

This text is of exceptional interest for students of Christian Origins, because it contains some remarkable parallels to a prediction about Jesus at the beginning of the Gospel of Luke. When the angel Gabriel appears to the Virgin Mary to announce the conception of Jesus, he tells her:

And now, you will conceive in your womb and bear a son, and you will name him Jesus. He will be great and will be called the Son of the Most High and the Lord God will give to him the throne of his ancestor David. He will reign over the house of Jacob forever, and of his kingdom there will be no end; . . . the child to be born will be holy; he will be called the Son of God. (Luke 1:31–35)

Three phrases are exact translation equivalents of phrases in the Aramaic text: "will be great," "he will be called Son of the Most High," and "he will be called Son of God."[48] If the Gospel of Luke showed parallels of this exactitude to a passage in the Prophets, no one would doubt that there was a literary allusion. It is hard to avoid the conclusion that Luke is dependent in some way on this text from Qumran.

In the New Testament text "Son of the Most High" and "Son of God" are clearly messianic titles: the Lord God will give to him the throne of his ancestor David. There has been considerable dispute, however, about the figure in the scroll (4Q246). As noted above, a space is left blank in the second column before the words "until the people of God arises." Some scholars, including Milik, have inferred that this is the turning point of the prophecy, and that everything prior to this point must be interpreted in a negative sense. So Milik suggested that the "Son of God" was a Syrian king, specifically

Alexander Balas, son of Antiochus Epiphanes.[49] Balas is called *theopator* (god-begotten) and *Deo patre natus* (born of a divine father) on coins. David Flusser suggested that he was the anti-Christ.[50] Geza Vermes has suggested that he was a usurper.[51] No Jewish text, however, applies such honorific titles to a usurper, or to a Syrian king. The Book of Daniel notes that Antiochus Epiphanes exalted himself and considered himself greater than any god (Dan. 11:36–39), but it makes quite clear that his claims were not justified. I have no doubt that the Son of the Most High is a positive figure in a Jewish text.

Those scholars who have looked for one clear turning point in the text have misunderstood the style in which it is written. The text bears a strong resemblance to apocalyptic writings, especially to the Book of Daniel, which it echoes with the phrases "his kingdom is an everlasting kingdom" (compare Dan. 3:33, 7:27) and "his sovereignty is an everlasting sovereignty" (compare Dan. 4:31, 7:13). Now it is typical of apocalyptic writings that they go over the same ground several times in slightly different ways. For example, Daniel 7 begins by describing Daniel's vision of the four beasts rising out of the sea, and the coming of one like a "son of man" on the clouds of heaven. Then there is a short interpretation by an angel, that the four beasts are four kings, and that the holy ones of the Most High will receive the kingdom. Then Daniel asks for clarification and gives a further description of part of the vision. This is followed by a further interpretation, which says that the kingdom will be given to the people of the holy ones of the Most High. In all, the "kingdom" is given three times, once to the one like a son of man, once to the holy ones of the Most High, and finally to the people of the holy ones of the Most High.

I would suggest that there is similar redundancy in the "Son of God" text. The affliction on earth, described in column 1, is followed by the coming of the "Son of God." Then the text reverts to the period of affliction, followed by the rise of the people of God. The coming of the Son of God and the rise of the people of God do not follow each other in sequence, but are two aspects of the same thing, like the one like a son of man and the holy ones of the Most High in Daniel.

If this is so, then the Son of God figure must be the representative of the people of God. He could conceivably be an angel, like the archangel Michael in Daniel,[52] but he is more likely to be the Messiah. There is a clear basis in the Hebrew Bible for referring to the anointed Davidic king as the son of God. Psalm 2 tells how the kings of the earth took counsel "against the Lord and his anointed" and goes on to "tell the decree of the Lord: He said to me "You are my son, today I have begotten you." The psalm, of course, was referring to the king of the day, but in the Dead Sea Scrolls all the psalms and prophets are understood to refer to the end of days. The idea that the king is son of God is also found in Nathan's oracle in 2 Sam. 7:14, in which the Lord promises that he will establish the kingdom of David's offspring: "I will be a father to him, and he shall be a son to me" (NRSV). This passage is interpreted in the Dead Sea Scrolls, in a document known as the *Florilegium:* "I [will be] his father and he shall be my son. He is the branch of David who shall arise with the Interpreter of the Law [to rule] in Zion [at the end] of time."[53] All these passages provide clear parallels for referring to the Messiah as the Son of God.

The expression "Son of God" acquired a new range of meaning in Christianity, where it was associated with the idea of a virgin birth, and eventually with a metaphysical status in the context of a Trinity. The close parallel between the "Son of God text" and the Gospel of Luke, however, reminds us that the expression was Jewish in origin and was a way of expressing the specially close relationship between the king and God. In the Hebrew Bible, the king is son of God by adoption. There is good reason to think that in early Christianity, too, "son of God" was originally an honorific title, which did not necessarily imply such notions as virgin birth or Trinitarian status.

The figure who is called "Son of God" here, however, fits well with the Branch of David Prince of the Congregation of the other Dead Sea Scrolls we have considered. He appears in the context of the final war. After his intervention there is peace. God makes war on his behalf, but the human king is no less a warrior for that. It is interesting, however, that the biblical background of this text is not Isaiah 11 or Numbers 24, or any of the texts cited in other messianic passages. Instead, the clearest allusions are to Daniel 7, where Daniel has his famous vision of "one like a son of man" coming on the clouds of heaven. For much of Jewish and Christian tradition the "son of man" was understood as the Davidic Messiah. It may be that the messianic interpretation of Daniel 7 is already implied in this fragmentary text from Qumran.[54]

THE MESSIAH OF HEAVEN AND EARTH (ON RESURRECTION, 4Q521)

The final text to be considered here is somewhat different from the others. Again, it is a very fragmentary text. The longest fragment reads as follows:

> ...the heavens and the earth will obey his messiah, [and all th]at is in them will not turn aside from the commandments of the Holy Ones. You who seek the Lord, strengthen yourselves in his service. Is it not in this that you will find the Lord, all who hope in their hearts. For the Lord will seek out the pious and call the righteous by name, and the spirit will hover over the poor and he will renew the faithful by his might. For he will glorify the pious on the throne of an eternal kingdom, releasing captives, giving sight to the blind and raising up those who are bo[wed down]. Forever I will cleave to [those who] hope, and in his kindness.... The fru[it of a] good [wor]k will not be delayed for anyone and the glorious things that have not taken place the Lord will do as he s[aid] for he will heal the wounded, give life to the dead and preach good news to the poor and he will [sat]isfy the [weak] ones and lead those who have been cast out and enrich the hungry....

Michael Wise and James Tabor have drawn attention to the similarity between this text and a passage in the Gospels.[55] When John the Baptist sends his disciples to ask Jesus "Are you the one who is to come, or should we look for another?" Jesus replies, "Go and report to John what you have seen and heard: the blind receive sight, the lame walk, the lepers are cleansed and the deaf hear, the dead are raised up, the poor have the glad tidings preached to them" (Matt. 11:4–5; Luke 7:22–23). The Gospels, of course, claim that Jesus raised the dead on a number of occasions. Wise and Tabor infer that the notion of a messiah who would raise the dead preceded Christianity and is attested in this fragmentary text from Qumran.

It is not possible here to address all the problems raised by this interesting text, but a few comments can be made.

First, while God is the grammatical subject of the verbs "heal," "give life," and so on, I am inclined to agree with Wise, however, that a human agent, rather than God, is likely to preach the glad tidings to the poor. In short God acts through an agent, but the acts are still the acts of God.

Second, if this is so, we must ask what manner of agent is envisaged. The motif of preaching glad tidings to the poor is taken from Isaiah 61:

> The spirit of the Lord God is upon me,
> because the Lord has anointed me;
> he has sent me to bring good news to the oppressed,
> to bind up the brokenhearted,
> to proclaim liberty to the captives,
> and release to the prisoners;
> to proclaim the year of the Lord's favor ...

The figure envisaged in Isaiah is a prophet, who acts as the messenger of the Lord. He is anointed, and so is a *Mashiah*. Another Qumran scroll that draws on Isaiah 61, the Melchizedek scroll, refers to the herald who preaches glad tidings as "the anointed of the spirit." The word "anointed" is also used with reference to the prophets in other documents from Qumran. It is perhaps worth noting that the plural form, "her anointed ones," occurs in another fragment of this composition, 4Q521.

Isaiah 61 does not say that the anointed figure will raise the dead. If we regard this figure as a prophet, however, there is an obvious precedent for raising the dead in the stories of Elijah and Elisha. Elijah was also expected to return at the end of days. At the beginning of this essay, we mentioned the passage in the *Rule of the Community* which speaks of the coming of the prophet and the messiahs of Aaron and Israel. I would suggest that the figure in 4Q521 is more likely to correspond to the prophet of that passage than to the messiahs of Aaron or Israel.[56] There is little if any royal imagery in the passage, and it does not correspond at all to the portrayals of a warlike prince of the congregation which we have seen consistently in other passages. Some scholars have questioned whether this is a sectarian text at all,[57] and indeed it lacks clear points of contact with other sectarian scrolls, with the possible exception of the Melchizedek scroll. There is notoriously little evidence for a belief in the raising of the dead in the sectarian Qumran corpus.[58]

None of this is to deny that 4Q521 provides a remarkable parallel to the New Testament. It shows, indeed, that the Gospel portrayals of Jesus were heavily dependent on Jewish expectations of the time, perhaps even more heavily than we had realized. It is also true that early Christianity was influenced by *sectarian* Judaism, especially by the strands of Judaism that were inclined to apocalypticism and eschatological expectation. However, our survey also shows that the relationship between Jewish and Christian messianic expectations was far from simple.

CONCLUSION

We have seen in the Dead Sea Scrolls a strong expectation of a Davidic messiah, the Messiah of Israel. His role was primarily that of a warrior. He was to re-establish the kingdom of Israel. His authority was subject to that of the high priest, at least in some respects. Some of the titles of this figure (Son of God, Son of the Most High) were taken over by early Christianity.

Jesus of Nazareth, however, did not qualify as a warrior messiah. It may be that some of his followers had expected him to restore the kingdom of Israel, but such expectations could not be maintained after his crucifixion. So in the Gospels the warlike character of the messiah fades into the background, to re-emerge only in the Book of Revelation. Instead, Jesus was seen as the fulfillment of various expectations, some of which we might associate with an eschatological prophet rather than the King Messiah, and some of which admitted of a heavenly, otherworldly character. The separate priestly messiah finds no place in early Christianity. Jesus himself would be portrayed as the heavenly High Priest in the Epistle to the Hebrews.

The Dead Sea Scrolls, then, do not uncover the sources of Christian messianism in any simple way. They do, however, throw much light on the subject. The Jewish followers of Jesus were different in many ways from the Dead Sea sect. They did not have such a strong priestly character, and were not so preoccupied with purity laws. Nonetheless they shared the same Scriptures, and tended to interpret them in similar ways. Both groups were part of the rich and varied fabric that made up Judaism around the turn of the era.

NOTES

1. See John J. Collins, *The Scepter and the Star: The Messiahs of the Dead Sea Scrolls and Other Ancient Literature* (New York: Doubleday, 1995); "Jesus and the Messiahs of Israel," in *Geschichte-Tradition-Reflexion: Festschrift für Martin Hengel,* ed. H. Lichtenberger (Tübingen: Mohr, 1996), 3:287–302; F. García Martínez, "Messianische Erwartungen in den Qumranschriften," *Jahrbuch für biblische Theologie* 8 (1993): 3–31.

2. See F. M. Cross, *The Ancient Library of Qumran and Modern Biblical Studies,* rev. ed. (Garden City, N.Y.: Doubleday, 1961), 14, and the literature there cited.

3. G. Vermes and M. Goodman, *The Essenes according to the Classical Sources* (Sheffield: JSOT, 1989).

4. See T. S. Beall, *Josephus' Description of the Essenes Illustrated by the Dead Sea Scrolls* (Cambridge: Cambridge University Press, 1988); J. J. Collins, "Essenes," *ABD* 2:619–26.

5. Josephus, *Jewish War* §160–61.

6. See J. M. Baumgarten, "The Qumran-Essene Restraints on Marriage," in *Archaeology and History in the Dead Sea Scrolls*, ed. L. H. Schiffman (Sheffield: JSOT, 1990), 13–24. Baumgarten notes that CD 7.6–7 ("and if they live in camps according to the order of the land and take wives and beget children…") may imply that not all members of the sect married.

7. N. Golb, "The Problem of Origin and Identification of the Dead Sea Scrolls," *Proceedings of the American Philosophical Society* 124 (1980): 1–24; Golb, "Who Hid the Dead Sea Scrolls," *BA* 28 (1987): 68–82; Golb, "The Dead Sea Scrolls," *The American Scholar* 58 (1989): 177–207; Golb, "Khirbet Qumran and the Manuscripts of the Judaean Wilderness: Observations on the Logic of Their Investigation," *JNES* 49 (1990): 103–14; Golb, *Who Wrote the Dead Sea Scrolls?* (New York: Macmillan, 1994). See the critique of Golb by F. García Martínez and A. S. van der Woude, "A 'Groningen' Hypothesis of Qumran Origins and Early History," *RevQ* 14 (1990): 526–41.

8. So P. Donceel-Voûte, "The Archaeology of Khirbet Qumran," in *Methods of Investigation of the Dead Sea Scrolls and the Khirbet Qumran Site: Present Realities and Future Prospects*, ed. M. O. Wise et al., Annals of the New York Academy of Sciences 722 (New York: New York Academy of Sciences, 1994), 1–32.

9. So Golb. The site had been identified as a military fort before the discovery of the scrolls (see Cross, *Ancient Library of Qumran*, 54).

10. Donceel-Voûte, "Archaeology of Khirbet Qumran," argued that the site was too luxurious for a quasimonastic settlement. She distinguishes a residential area and an industrial area on the site. The evidence for luxury (glass, some fine pottery, urns, and stone work) is quite limited, however. At the same conference, J. Magness emphasized the scarcity of fine ware at Qumran in her paper on "The Community at Qumran in Light of Its Pottery," in *Methods of Investigation*, 39–50. See now J. Magness, "What Was Qumran? Not a Country Villa," *BARev* 22 (1996): 37–47, 72–73.

11. J. T. Milik, in his review of P. Wernberg-Moller, *The Manual of Discipline Translated and Annotated, with an Introduction*, in *RB* 67 (1960): 411, claimed that this passage was missing from the earliest copy of the Rule. This is now disputed by L. Schiffman, who claims that the "omission" is due to the joining of two separate fragments. See the clarification by J. H. Charlesworth, "From Messianology to Christology: Problems and Prospects," in *The Messiah: Developments in Earliest*

Judaism and Christianity, ed. J. H. Charlesworth (Minneapolis: Fortress, 1992), 26–27.

12. K. G. Kuhn, "The Two Messiahs of Aaron and Israel," in *The Scrolls and the New Testament,* ed. K. Stendahl (New York: Harper, 1957), 54–64; J. Liver, "The Doctrine of the Two Messiahs in Sectarian Literature in the Time of the Second Commonwealth," *HTR* 52 (1969): 149–85; S. Talmon, "Waiting for the Messiah — The Conceptual World of the Qumran Covenanters," in *The World of Qumran from Within* (Leiden: Brill, 1989), 290–93.

13. CD 12.22–13.1; CD 14.18–19; CD 19.10–11 and 19.33–20:1). See L. Ginzberg, *An Unknown Jewish Sect,* trans. of 1922 German ed. (New York: Jewish Theological Seminary, 1976), and now M. Broshi, ed., *The Damascus Document Reconsidered* (New York: Israel Exploration Society, 1992).

14. See A. S. van der Woude, *Die messianische Vorstellungen der Gemeinde von Qumrân* (Assen: van Gorcum, 1957), 29.

15. M. Abegg, "The Messiah at Qumran: Are We Still Seeing Double?" *Dead Sea Discoveries* 2 (1995): 125–44.

16. CD 2.12, 6.1; 1QM 11.7.

17. On the Messiah in later Jewish tradition see G. Scholem, *On the Messianic Idea in Judaism* (New York: Schocken, 1971); L. Landman, ed., *Messianism in the Talmudic Era* (New York: Ktav, 1979). J. Neusner, *Messiah in Context* (Philadelphia: Fortress, 1984), emphasizes the limited role of the Messiah in the rabbinic corpus.

18. See L. H. Schiffman, *The Eschatological Community of the Dead Sea Scrolls* (Atlanta: Scholars Press, 1989), 53–67.

19. Translation by Charlesworth in *Rule of the Community and Related Documents,* ed. Charlesworth et al., Princeton Theological Seminary Dead Sea Scrolls Project 1 (Tübingen: J. C. B. Mohr [Paul Siebeck]; Louisville: Westminster/John Knox Press, 1994), 1:117.

20. See further J. VanderKam, "Messianism in the Scrolls," in *The Community of the Renewed Covenant: The Notre Dame Symposium on the Dead Sea Scrolls,* ed. E. Ulrich and J. VanderKam (Notre Dame, Ind.: University of Notre Dame Press, 1994), 211–34.

21. G. Vermes, *The Dead Sea Scrolls in English,* 4th ed. (Harmondsworth: Penguin, 1995), 321.

22. So M. Fishbane, "Use, Authority, and Interpretation of Mikra at Qumran," in *Mikra, Text, Translation: Reading and Interpretation of the Hebrew Bible in Ancient Judaism and Early Christianity,* ed. M. J. Mulder (Philadelphia: Fortress, 1988), 365; M. O. Wise, *A Critical Study of the Temple Scroll from Qumran Cave 11* (Chicago: Oriental Institute of the University of Chicago, 1990), 200.

23. Temple Scroll 56.20–21.

24. Translation by Charlesworth and L. T. Stuckenbruck, *Rule of the Community and Related Documents,* ed. Charlesworth, 1:129.

25. Translation by Charlesworth and Stuckenbruck, in ibid., 1: 130–31.

26. For its use in the Targumim see S. H. Levey, *The Messiah: An Aramaic Interpretation* (Cincinnati: Hebrew Union College, 1974), 21–27.

27. P. Borgen, "There Shall Come Forth a Man: Reflections on Messianic Ideas in Philo," in *The Messiah,* ed. Charlesworth, 341–61.

28. *y. Ta'anith* 68d. See G. Vermes, *Jesus the Jew* (Philadelphia: Fortress, 1981), 134.

29. B. Isaac and A. Oppenheimer, "Bar Kokhba," *ABD* 1:600.

30. 4Q161 (*Pesher on Isaiah*); 4Q174 (Florilegium); 4Q252 (*Patriarchal Blessings*).

31. 4Q252 (*Patriarchal Blessings*).

32. See Vermes, *Jesus the Jew,* 129–34; J. J. Collins, "Messiahs in Context: Method in the Study of Messianism in the Dead Sea Scrolls," in Wise et al., eds., *Methods of Investigation,* 213–29.

33. See Levey, *The Messiah.*

34. It is given as fragment 7 in R. H. Eisenman and M. Wise, *The Dead Sea Scrolls Uncovered* (Rockport, Mass.: Element, 1992), 28.

35. Ibid., 29.

36. G. Vermes, "The Oxford Forum for Qumran Research Seminar on the Rule of War from Cave 4 (4Q 285)," *JJS* 43 (1992): 85–90; M. Bockmuehl, "A 'Slain Messiah' in 4Q Serekh Milhamah (4Q 285)?," *Tyndale Bulletin* 43 (1992): 155–69; M. Abegg, "Messianic Hope and 4Q285: A Reassessment," *JBL* 113 (1994): 81–91.

37. In 4 Ezra 7:29, written about 100 C.E., the messiah dies peacefully after four hundred years. For the later tradition of a Messiah son of Joseph, or of Ephraim, see Vermes, *Jesus the Jew,* 139–40. This tradition is associated with Zech. 12:10 ("they shall look on him whom they have pierced").

38. The *New York Times* and the *Times* on Nov. 8, 1991, the *Chicago Tribune* on Nov. 11, 1991, and the *Independent* on Dec. 27, 1991.

39. See R. A. Horsley, "Messianic Figures and Movements in First-Century Palestine," in *The Messiah,* ed. Charlesworth, 276–95.

40. J. Heinemann, "The Messiah of Ephraim and the Premature Exodus of the Tribe of Ephraim," *HTR* 68 (1975): 1–15 (reprinted in *Messianism in the Talmudic Era,* ed. Landman, 339–53).

41. So J. H. Charlesworth, "Sense or Sensationalism? The Dead Sea Scrolls Controversy," *Christian Century* (January 29, 1992): 97.

42. J. T. Milik, "Milkî-sedeq et Milkîršea dans les écrits juives et chrétiens," *JJS* 23 (1972): 143.

43. P. R. Davies, "War Rule (1QM)," *ABD* 6875; E. P. Sanders,

Judaism, Practice and Belief, 63 B.C.E.–*66* C.E. (Philadelphia: Trinity, 1992), 296.

44. J. A. Fitzmyer, "The Contribution of Qumran Aramaic to the Study of the New Testament," *NTS* 20 (1973–74): 382–407; reprinted in his *A Wandering Aramean: Collected Aramaic Essays* (Missoula, Mont.: Scholars Press, 1977), 85–113.

45. D. Flusser, "The Hubris of the Antichrist in a Fragment from Qumran," *Immanuel* 10 (1980): 31–37; reprinted in his *Judaism and the Origins of Christianity* (Jerusalem: Magnes, 1988), 207–13; F. García Martínez, *Qumran and Apocalyptic: Studies on the Aramaic Texts from Qumran* (Leiden: Brill, 1992), 162–79.

46. E. Puech, "Fragment d'une Apocalypse en Araméen (4Q246 = pseudo-Dan) et le 'Royaume de Dieu,' " *RB* 99 (1992): 98–131; "Apocryphe de Daniel," in G. Brooke et al., *Qumran Cave 4. XVII. Parabiblical Texts, Part 3*, DJD 22 (Oxford: Clarendon, 1996), 165–84.

47. A transcription and translation can be found in Eisenman and Wise, *Dead Sea Scrolls Uncovered*, 70–71.

48. See Fitzmyer, *The Gospel according to Luke I–IX*, Anchor Bible 28 (Garden City, N.Y.: Doubleday, 1981), 205–6, 347–48.

49. See Puech, "Fragment," 123. E. M. Cook, "4Q246," *Bulletin for Biblical Research* 5 (1995): 43–66, argues that the reference is to Antiochus Epiphanes.

50. D. Flusser, "The Hubris of the Antichrist in a Fragment from Qumran," in Flusser, *Judaism and the Origins of Christianity* (Jerusalem: Magnes, 1988), 207–13.

51. Vermes, "Qumran Forum Miscellanea I," *JJS* 43 (1992): 303.

52. So García Martínez, *Qumran and Apocalyptic,* 243.

53. See G. J. Brooke, *Exegesis at Qumran: 4QFlorilegium in Its Jewish Context* (Sheffield: JSOT, 1985), 205.

54. See further my article, "The 'Son of God' Text from Qumran," in *From Jesus to John: Essays on Jesus and Christology in Honour of Marinus de Jonge,* ed. M. de Boer (Sheffield: JSOT, 1993), 65–82; and my *Scepter and the Star,* 154–94.

55. "The Messiah at Qumran," *BARev* 18.6 (Nov.–Dec. 1992): 65; "4Q521 'On Resurrection' and the Synoptic Gospel Tradition: A Preliminary Study," *JSP* 10 (1992): 149–62.

56. See J. J. Collins, "The Works of the Messiah," *Dead Sea Discoveries* 1 (1995): 98–112.

57. Vermes, "Qumran Forum Miscellanea I," 303–4.

58. Pace E. Puech, *La Croyance des Ésséniens en la vie future: immortalité, résurrection, vie éternelle* (Paris: Gabalda, 1993). See J. J. Collins, *Apocalypticism in the Dead Sea Scrolls* (London: Routledge, 1997), 110–29.

Chapter 3

Prophecy in the Dead Sea Scrolls

David Noel Freedman

The word "prophecy" has led a perilous existence. It has assumed a wide array of meanings, ranging from the flat equation with predicting the indefinite future to the speaking forth of a divine message intended only for the prophet's contemporaries. Still today this variety of practice can be seen in different religious communities. Somewhere along that continuum there also lay the usage of the early Christian and Qumran communities. Did these have anything in common in their usage? How did each think of itself as the heir or continuator of Hebrew prophecy? Let us look at these matters in turn, beginning first with a brief overview of prophecy in the tradition of the Hebrew Bible.

PROPHECY IN THE HEBREW BIBLE

Many issues can be debated and discussed, but I want to try to characterize the essential features of biblical prophecy from the ground level: How did people feel about this phenomenon, and what did they think prophecy was all about? The basic answer, the element that we can locate in all the prophets, is what the word means: prediction. Prophets were expected to predict. Now, however, the operational theory behind prediction was contact with God. The prophet was not supposed so much *merely* to predict as to convey a message. Whatever the message happened to be there was the firm conviction, the absolutely clear understanding that a prophet did not speak in his own right. The sole duty of a prophet was to convey the word of God. This is so central to biblical religion as to constitute the single, indispensable, necessary component. And there is an inseparable bond between this notion of prophecy and the written Bible, because the people who wrote it, organized it, produced it, and published it wanted the readers to understand that what they had written down ultimately traced back to the words that the prophet communicated, because the word of God is central to the whole story from the very beginning to the very end.

Consider the first chapter of Genesis. All is very clear regarding the whole of creation and the mechanism of its creation. God speaks and something happens. This way of doing things is rather unique among ancient ways of thinking about such things. The usual Near Eastern parallels almost always involve some handling or manipulation, and, of course, even in the second chapter of Genesis, God makes human beings out of clay. So it is perfectly possible for God to create humans in any number of ways, but in Genesis 1 it is done by the word: God speaks. Now that is the same word that the prophet speaks, because according to Isa. 55:8–11, especially verse 11, the word of God proceeds from God in heaven, and is active in the world. And this word is creative; it creates something that may be exactly its own content. That is the objective. It sets in motion a series of actions that produce results that come from the word; these results may not be the same as the word itself. But it is powerful and active, which is the point I am trying to emphasize. Prophecy, then, is central to the Bible from beginning to end, and the requirement, of course, is to have a prophet.

It is also true that there are not many authentic prophets.

Genuine ones do not come in regular sequence. One of the major problems in the Bible is that for every true prophet there are many false prophets. This point is evident, if perhaps also slightly exaggerated, in the story of Elijah at Mount Carmel, in his contest with the prophets of Baal. We know that the prophets of Baal are all false prophets because by definition all other gods are false and their prophets, all 450 of them, must also be false. Elijah keeps emphasizing that "I am absolutely the only one left," and later at Mount Horeb God reminds him that he is not. There are seven thousand other faithful Israelites who have not bowed the knee to Baal (and actually have not been quite as talkative either). At the same time, not many of them would have been prophets. Thus sorting out false and true prophets by this criterion of zealous fidelity is not easy, and there are other criteria. Since some prophets perform miracles and others do not, that is not an obligatory aspect of a true prophet. A true prophet is extremely significant and valuable, and, therefore, the words that the prophet utters are equally important.

This leads to a second point about the words of the prophet. Here we can invoke legal theory on the one hand and literary theory on the other hand. What is the significance of the text once it has been set down? Where do you go from there? When we turn to the Dead Sea Scrolls we find that the words of true prophets preserved in scripture, established as canonical and authoritative, basically are too valuable just to preserve. They were uttered in a certain context and they fit into a certain historical framework, but that has all passed. Is this just a record or does this have some kind of vitality? The idea is that the words of God, once spoken, keep resonating, keep reverberating. The question is, "What do you do with them?" Those words become very important when you do not have a living prophet. The tradition in early rabbinic Judaism is that after Ezra and Nehemiah, after the closing of the canon, which ostensibly went back to the great synagogue, there were no more prophets. With the latest prophets, like Haggai, Zechariah, and Malachi, the list was closed. Consequently, if there is no living prophet to give answers, the next best thing is recycling the old prophecies. If the right interpreter is available, that is, an established, authoritative interpreter, then scriptural prophecy still has vitality. If there is no prophet, there must be someone who knows how to interpret older prophecy, and, even more, to interpret, apply it, and bring it up to date. That process is not dissimilar from what modern preachers do from week to week in churches: take the Bible and apply it. That is really what was going on at Qumran. We know that the Righteous Teacher (*mōrēh haṣṣedeq*), was their *inspired interpreter*. The theory of the powerful interpreter is spelled out more in detail in the Qumran texts than anywhere in the Bible. Someone with the right credentials, who is guided by the spirit of God, can take an ancient prophecy and recycle it.

TWO KINDS OF PROPHECY

Basically there are two kinds of prophecy in the Hebrew Bible, but there is also a spectrum, so that there are varying proportions of each kind in the group. First, there are prophecies that are explicit and time-bound. A prophet says that something is going to happen soon, the next day or the next year; the normal time limit is two years, as specific statements by prophets or other indicators make clear. Sometimes the prophets are less precise, or more hazy, to give themselves some leeway or breathing space. If the time limit is flexible, then more prophecies can be supported or maintained. The prophecy may not have been fulfilled within a narrow range, but if one allows more time, then it may yet be fulfilled. One of the more explicit prophets was a man named Hananiah, a contemporary of Jeremiah. Hananiah may be designated as a false prophet, because we are told that his prophecy about the Temple vessels, which had been carted off to Babylonia by Nebuchadnezzar, did not come true; and as we all know, there is no Book of Hananiah in the Bible. A direct confrontation between Hananiah and the (true) prophet Jeremiah is recorded in the Book of Jeremiah (Jeremiah 28). When this event took place, the audience did not have the benefit of hindsight, as we do; we know which one was the true prophet and which one the false.

What was the confrontation about? When Nebuchadnezzar, the great Babylonian king, captured Jerusalem (spring, 597 B.C.E.), he took the sacred vessels and other utensils back to Babylon. A few years later (c. 594 B.C.E.), Hananiah announced that all of these vessels would be brought back to Jerusalem, specifically "within two years." Jeremiah did not contest the truth of the prophecy, just the timing. Although he ultimately branded the prophecy and the prophet as false, his basic contention was that the desired result could not occur within two years, or even within the lifetime of those then living. For Jeremiah, the time frame had to be not less than a life-span of seventy years, before the vessels or even any of the captives (i.e., their offspring) could return to the homeland. Not before seventy years had passed would any Jews return from exile. We know that nothing happened within the two-year period specified by Hananiah, and by that time Hananiah was already dead, following a specific prediction by Jeremiah that the other prophet would not live out the year in which he made the prophecy. While we might regard the premature demise of Hananiah as a curious coincidence, in that day the event would have been understood as divine punishment of the false prophet for misleading the people.[1] In any case, we see in this episode between Hananiah and Jeremiah what the general and popular perception of predictive prophecy was.

Consider another specific prediction, perhaps the most famous of all, the prediction concerning the birth of a male child made by the prophet Isaiah around 735/734 B.C.E. (Isa. 7:14). There can be little question that insofar as the prophet himself was concerned, he was talking about an event that would occur within a very short time, within a few years at most. In this case, the prophecy was fulfilled literally, but ever since the rise of Christianity, hardly anyone remembers what the original occasion was, or what the prophet Isaiah had in mind when he made the prophecy. He was talking about a war then going on, with Israel and Aram (=modern Syria) united against Judah. The armies of the two northern nations had invaded the southern country, and were already threatening the capital city of Jerusalem. In this crisis, the prophet met with Ahaz, the king of Judah, and assured him that within a short time — a few years at most, specifically before the child that the young woman is going to bear is old enough to distinguish good from bad — the war would be over and the issues raised by it would be resolved in favor of Judah. In other words, Isaiah was insisting that there was nothing for the king to worry about.[2] Although the time range given by the prophet was not specific, the range was limited, and depended upon how long it took a child to learn the difference between right and wrong, or what was regarded as the age of responsibility (it was not a matter of "bar-mitzvah," which is postbiblical, but of answerability, which began much earlier, perhaps as young as two or three, and certainly was attained by six or seven).

A little later on, Isaiah called attention to another child, his own son, whom he named *Maher-Shalal-Hash-Baz*, which means, "Spoil hastens, Booty speeds." The prophet was referring to the same war, only this time the range of prediction is even more restricted. Before this child is old enough to cry out "father" or "mother," the war will end in disaster for the invaders (Isa. 8:1–4). Here the time frame cannot be more than a year or so. Hence we are dealing with explicit and specific prophecies. And both were fulfilled. Within two or three years the Assyrians came from the east, conquered the Aramaean kingdom of Damascus, and successfully invaded Israel, but did *not* take Jerusalem because of a plague (2 Kings 18:13–19:37; 2 Chron. 32:1–20; Isa. 36:1–37:38). Aram was turned into an Assyrian province, while Israel was reduced to the status of client kingdom, only to be overrun yet again within the decade and turned into provinces of the Assyrian Empire (between 732 and 722 B.C.E.).

Then there are prophecies with no specific date, which are

harder to deal with. For example, the prophet Ezekiel is accused by his countrymen, his fellow exiles, of deliberately extending the time frame, of being vague and hazy, to protect himself from making false predictions. Ezekiel is disturbed by this charge, and promises that in the future his prophecies will have a deadline, a terminal date, and be specific.[3] This accusation and response reflect a problem with prophecy not easily overcome. There are many other prophecies with introductory headings, such as, "In the last days," "At the end of days," "The days are coming," all of which signify that the prediction concerns the end-time, which is always near, but also never quite happens, at least not a fulfillment in literal terms of the extravagant language of the predictions.

PROPHECY AT QUMRAN

The people at Qumran believed that they were living in the last days, and that is the key to their use of prophecy. They thought that prophecies of all types were going to come true in the very near future, and many other prophecies, seemingly time-bound, would also come true in different ways, according to the authoritative interpretation and adaptation of the inspired Righteous Teacher.

I want to repeat this point, namely, that revelation from God is central to the Hebrew Bible and the community or communities that accepted it as authoritative. The means or mechanisms by which revelation was received and transmitted, and then preserved, were the prophets and their prophecies, and their amanuenses (like Baruch for Jeremiah). Most prophets in the Hebrew Bible have dreams, or visions and auditions; they see things and hear words. Moses is special; he is the classic prophet. God speaks to him face to face as a person speaks to a friend (Exod. 33:11; Num. 12:8; Deut. 34:10). In the case of Moses, the emphasis is on the reality and reliability of the communication, just as ordinary and natural as a conversation between friends — only one of the participants is God himself. The conviction that God really spoke to Moses and the other prophets, and that the communication was authentic and vitally important, and that the words are powerfully and permanently active in the world — such a conviction dominates the thinking of the biblical communities and, specifically, the people of Qumran.[4]

For the people of Qumran, the best thing would have been to have a true prophet in their midst to give them direct revelation from God, and daily instruction as to how to live and what to do in preparation for the great and terrible day of the Lord, which was imminent. Lacking such an authentic prophet, they had the next best thing, the presence of an inspired and authoritative interpreter of prophecies already delivered and enshrined in the canonical text of the Hebrew Bible. In other words, when new contemporary prophetic utterances are unavailable or unacceptable, the alternative is to recycle the old prophecies. This is achieved by an authoritative interpreter, who takes the canonical prophecies and interprets and applies them to the current situation, not anticipated by the earlier prophet, but creatively connected with the contemporary scene by the leading teacher. Thus is produced a derivative but authoritative interpretation of the older text, and it is the application that displaces the original for all practical purposes.

As I observed, the Qumranites believed they were in the last days and, therefore, not only were all the prophecies of the last days applicable and appropriate, but the scribes at Qumran extended this assumption by writing commentaries on many books. Practically every book of scripture would be available for reapplication. And we have explicit commentaries not only on the prophetic books like Habakkuk, but also on the Psalms and other books. We find the same pattern in the New Testament; whether the quotation or citation is actually a prophetic word or not does not really matter, everything is potentially prophetic.

There is a connection here with modern literary and legal theory. Recall, for example, the constitutional debate a few years ago over the nomination of Robert Bork as candidate for the Supreme Court. The key words in that debate were "original intent." Bork's theory of how the Supreme Court should function was that it should evaluate statutes, cases, and so on, on the basis not only of the words of the Constitution, but of what the framers of the Constitution intended when they wrote it. That seems very reasonable and is part of general literary theory. One thing to take into account is what the author meant when he or she wrote the words. This turned out to be a serious bone of contention because a contrary theory says that the function of the Supreme Court is to *adapt* the Constitution, which, after all, was written in the eighteenth century, to conditions, circumstances, and cases in the twentieth century. Very often specific matters are at issue which the founding fathers not only never mentioned, but could hardly have thought about. What is to be done? Because the Constitution was devised for the country, it was intended to be used not only while the authors were alive but beyond their time as well.

This could lead us to the subject of textuality, about which so much is being said and written these days in biblical studies. We could inquire into such things as authorial intent, textuality, intertextuality, intratextuality, and reader response. But I shall be content here with observing that a very important school of thought says that once the text leaves the hand of the author it is no longer his or hers. Copyright law grants ownership for the author's lifetime and fifty years thereafter. But ultimately, both legally and literarily, the work is out of the author's hands. After the copyright expires, legally anyone can do anything with it and, according to the Qumran people, everything is up to the interpreter, which is what modern literary theory says as well. In other words, the reader or the critic decides what something means. That strikes me as a little scary.

At Qumran an authoritative interpreter, such as the Community's Teacher, can tell you what a biblical text really means, in terms of the Community's own situation. Take the *Commentary* (=*Pesher*) *on Habakkuk*. First of all, what is the book of Habakkuk about? Without going into all the controversial questions, we can say that ostensibly the prophet Habakkuk is speaking out of and back into the international situation of his own day, when the Chaldeans, led by their kings, Nabopolassar and his son the famous Nebuchadnezzar II, conquered most of the Near East, and established the so-called Neo-Babylonian Empire (Nebuchadnezzar reigned from 605 until 562 B.C.E.). Habakkuk, stationed in Judah, is an observer of the international scene, and specifically of the violent conquest of so many nations, including Judah, by the Chaldeans, and he raises important theological and ethical questions with God, as he describes the invasion and conquest by these vast forces.

The Qumran commentary, while quoting the text in a generally reliable fashion, unit by unit, nevertheless ignores or dismisses the historical setting and context of the prophetic book. It reinterprets the contents and applies them to an entirely different historical situation, in which the people of Qumran find themselves, approximately five hundred years later. The Chaldeans have long since come and gone, but now there is a new conquering invader, and an adjustment is necessary in order to accommodate the new developments. The hermeneutical device, in this case, is the substitution of the name of the new conquering empire in place of the old one, and then the prophecies can be recycled and reused. Instead of the Chaldeans, the subject is the Kittites (in Hebrew, the word *Kaśdîm* = Chaldeans is replaced by *Kittiyyîm* = Kittites). The latter term refers to the Greek successors of Alexander the Great, who established kingdoms in Syria (the Seleucids) and Egypt (the Ptolemies). What lies behind the transposition from *Kaśdîm* to *Kittiyyîm* is the conviction that the ancient prophecy did not exhaust its content or its power in the earlier history, but is now to be fulfilled more fully and completely, in fact finally and absolutely. The interpreters at Qumran believed and argued further that God always intended these words to apply to their contemporary situation, quite apart from the prophet's own understanding of the meaning and application of the words (in his day).

There is a certain irony in the fact that the description in the book of Habakkuk fits the *Kittiyyîm* quite well; at least one prominent scholar believed that the book of Habakkuk was a product of the hellenistic age, and that it was originally written about the *Kittiyyîm,* and then retroverted to the Chaldean period as part of an elaborate rewriting of Israelite history and prophecy.[5] There is no merit in this hypothesis, but it illustrates how adaptable prophetic words are to different historical situations. The underlying reason is that the basic pattern of conquest does not vary much, and the overall picture is much the same, while the details may vary. It should be observed, however, that the same words can be applied to any number of historical situations, with greater or lesser accuracy. So while the application to the *Kittiyyîm* of the words of Habakkuk is clever and deft, it is not necessarily more appropriate to that particular situation than it might have been to other historical developments in other periods. Thus, if the procedure was merely one of homiletical or hortatory adaptation, one might read with appreciation and admiration and then go on to other matters. We could hardly object to such a procedure, as it has been the stock in trade of commentators and preachers for millennia, and specifically in reference to the text of the Bible. The process of reinterpretation and adaptation is both necessary and helpful in understanding and applying the text to the changing human situation.

A problem arises, however, when a specific interpretation and application are accorded special, even unique status, as the only authentic and authoritative and therefore the only valid interpretation and application of the text being considered. Thus the *Habakkuk Commentary* is not merely an example of clever exegesis and creative analysis, but the exclusively authoritative interpretation of this material from scripture, and affirms this interpretation only, against all others, including past and any possible future ones. There can be only one right interpretation, and this one is it.

From our perspective, that is carrying things a bit too far, especially as different groups at different times and places have interpreted scripture in a similar way, but applied the same texts to entirely different situations in very different historical circumstances. These are examples of reader response, in critical theory, that go beyond acceptable limits.

At Qumran there is no freedom of interpretive choice; one must believe and obey the interpretation given as proper discipline and as adherence to the veritable word of God. That combination of discipline and demand for absolute obedience is volatile and dangerous. We can surely admire how clever, how ingenious, and how apropos this kind of prophetic adaptation can be. I think they carried it off very well. And it gives one a sense of immediacy and a powerful impact when words written down four or five hundred years earlier are interpreted in this fashion. Preachers would be delighted to achieve a result like that. Hence we can be duly respectful and admire this kind of work, but also recognize what is happening and the inherent dangers in the process. The experience and fate of the numerous apocalyptic movements in the United States in the nineteenth century, which pinned their hopes and expectations on specific dates and events (all of which were disappointed) can serve as an example of insisting on absolute and unique control of truth in interpreting scripture. The ascendancy of fundamentalist groups in all the major religious communities in our own times, and the intolerance of different and divergent opinions, do not bode well for the future of humanity.

THE SCROLLS AND THE NEW TESTAMENT

With these flashers and warnings let us turn to the New Testament. The Habakkuk Scroll immediately revealed that the Qumran Community had a system of interpretation of scripture very much like what we find in the New Testament. The basic difference is that the Qumran people did it systematically, by taking whole books, or big parts of books, dealing with the

Hebrew books verse by verse and chapter by chapter, whereas the New Testament writers gave quotations, citations, a verse here or a verse there, maybe two verses or three verses, from different parts of the whole. In other words there is a different way of arranging things, but the system is essentially the same, and both are construed as authoritative and inspired interpretations of the scriptures. The attitude is the same, that these are the last days, the fulfillment of prophecy is now taking place, and what matters is to find the correct prophecy, interpret it correctly, and then write it down. And we know, as I have already mentioned, that classic examples of this procedure appear all over the New Testament. The New Testament seems to reflect a situation different from what we have at Qumran, where dedicated Jews focused attention on one inspired interpreter, and who provided authoritative explanations and applications of scripture. In the New Testament we have information about new prophets — John the Baptist, Jesus himself, John (in Revelation), and then a whole class in the early church. These people get the message directly from God (or Christ) and speak to continuing life situations. For example, both John the Baptist and Jesus are credited with predicting the coming of the end. And in Jesus' case, it is spelled out, especially in the last chapters of Mark and Matthew and Luke, in the so-called little apocalypse, the coming of the end in and around Jerusalem, the destruction of the Temple, the city, and other related matters. Certainly the claim is made that Jesus and John were both authentic prophets, chiefly because they made predictions that were fulfilled. Along with prophets speaking directly to the situation, there remains this vast literature from the Hebrew Bible that is used to identify, to clarify, to explain, and to drive home the point that what is happening in these days with Jesus and the disciples, and after that with Peter and Paul (Acts), is in accordance with ancient prophecy, and fulfills the prophetic content. The classic virgin birth prophecy from Matthew comes from the Book of Isaiah, in which we can date both the prophecy and its fulfillment. But the theory is that words like that have an indefinite shelf life; they can be used anytime and they continue to exert power and force and influence. All that was just too much of a connection for a writer like Matthew to overlook. The evangelists or inspired interpreters do not create events; they get the events through tradition, or other sources that they record. Not all such events might withstand the scrutiny of modern science or history, but given the character of the transmission and these other factors, basically the writers are not creating events out of the Hebrew Bible; they are using the Hebrew Bible to connect the events with a divine plan. All these things that happened to Jesus and the disciples, from beginning to end, including the death and resurrection, have already been anticipated, and all that is needed for proper understanding is the correct guide. The story then comes through not just as a series of unrelated events, but as a coherent whole connected by the prophetic utterances that convey the plan of God.

CONCLUSION

The methods used by the New Testament writers correspond very closely to what we find at Qumran; only the details vary. In other words these communities respectively have a structure in which there is one or more — there could be many — authorized interpreters. And the acceptance of their interpretations, of their applications, is part of the canonical process. There is hardly any question that the commentaries at Qumran were regarded as authoritative for the life of the Community, whether it was a matter of belief or of practice. They were not simply another interpretation or another option. Most of us could recognize the validity of that. Any piece of literature — prophetic, poetic — can bear different gradations of analysis or of interpretation. Critics differ over something that was published yesterday. How much more so over something two thousand years old? In other words, there are all kinds of variations and possibilities, but which one is right? We have a problem here. We have already ruled out the author's intention as the ultimate guide, as he was not fully inspired about his own words, the words of God. Whose words, then, are authoritative? The authoritative interpreter, the Righteous Teacher, is the one who has the right words. That interpretation then becomes *the* interpretation.

Now we know that the people of Qumran were in rather bitter debate with others, with what we can call the establishment, with the consequence that the Qumran Community necessarily offered a choice to the would-be member: If you wish to join us, then you must take our interpretation; the other people are just wrong, plain wrong! We can imagine a situation like this benignly and with objectivity. We can evaluate the Qumranites with some sympathy, count up the positive and negative aspects of their labors and their achievements, in the framework of their understanding of the Bible and how they recycled and reinterpreted biblical prophecy. But what do we do about the New Testament and the church, which composed its interpretation and made it the authoritative interpretation of the Hebrew Bible?

In the New Testament, we find new prophecy, which we can test by established means, but in addition, much of the Hebrew Bible is mined for data that are used to support New Testament assertions and claims. And most of these claims and assertions are in classic opposition to the traditional Jewish understanding and interpretation of the same scriptures. The words are mainly the same, but the meaning and sense are often quite different.

Jewish and Christian interpretations of the same materials vary widely. That circumstance raises what I regard as a real issue. We may observe this phenomenon in the Dead Sea Scrolls as an interesting variation on or deviation from normal standards of historical and linguistic exegesis and not be seriously concerned, except in an academic way. But between church and synagogue there are almost two thousand years of radically different and divergent analysis and polemics about the meaning and use of the Hebrew Bible. Is it possible to end the warfare and come to some understanding or accommodation? Can there be an exegesis and interpretation that is neither Jewish nor Christian, but scholarly and objective, and at the same time serve both church and synagogue better than their private interpretations of the past? Or should we agree that Jewish and Christian approaches and applications have separate and equally honorable and acceptable places in the mosaic built out of the effects of time and circumstance? Which way lies the future of biblical studies?

NOTES

1. Consider the punishment to be meted out to false prophets in Deut. 18:15–22, especially v. 20; also the curious story of the death of Pelatiah in Ezek. 11:1–13, especially v. 13; the two episodes in Jeremiah 28 and Ezekiel 11 are dated within two years of each other.

2. There are some interpretive questions in the text, e.g., the Hebrew word for "young woman" is *almah*, a female of childbearing age. Also the Hebrew verb translated "going to bear" is slightly ambiguous, and could be interpreted to mean that the woman in question is already pregnant, or is expected to be — more likely the former, as she seems to be present on the occasion. If not actually pregnant, then she might be expected to become so within a very short time. Annual pregnancies were hardly uncommon in that society in those days.

3. Cf. Ezek. 12:21–28, especially vv. 27–28: "Son of man, behold the house of Israel are saying, 'The vision that he sees is for many days (ahead) and for distant times he is prophesying.' Therefore, say to them, 'Thus has said my Lord Yahweh, None of my words will be drawn out any longer; whenever I speak a word, then it shall be accomplished!' Oracle of my Lord Yahweh."

4. Cf. Isa. 55:10–11; also Isa. 40:8.

5. Cf. C. C. Torrey, "The Prophecy of Habakkuk," *Jewish Studies in Memory of George A. Kohut, 1874–1933*, ed. S. W. Baron and A. Marx (New York: Alexander Kohut Memorial Foundation, 1935), 565–82. He was not the only one, however. Cf. the discussion by G. Fohrer in his *Introduction to the Old Testament*, trans. D. E. Green (Nashville: Abingdon, 1968), 451–56, esp. 454–55.

Chapter 4

The Dead Sea Scrolls
and Christian Faith

James H. Charlesworth

The media have helped make the Dead Sea Scrolls a household word. Many people are fascinated by these ancient scrolls; some of them are not usually interested in religious issues. Immediately after the sensational controversy over the Dead Sea Scrolls in the early 1990s, the unpublished fragments could be seen by virtually anyone. Subsequently, two professors claimed in November 1991 that they had discovered a fragment that referred to the Messiah who had *died for the sins of the world*. They claimed that these scrolls represented virtually an early form of "Christianity"; that is, the claims of Jesus' earliest followers seemed to be found in these long-lost ancient Hebrew fragments.

John Noble Wilford of the *New York Times* called me to ask if I had seen the fragment labeled 4Q285, that is, a series of fragments found in Qumran Cave 4 to which scroll experts gave the number 285. The answer was "yes." He then asked what it said. I replied that the word "Messiah" appeared on the fragment, but it seemed more likely that he killed some people than that he was killed. The original document is now preserved only by seven fragments, averaging only about seven fragmented lines each. There are no words that can be interpreted "for the sins of the world." These were added by the translator to fill in holes in the leather. The discussions over this tiny piece of a scroll thousands of years old caused a brouhaha: some Christians were alarmed, but others were afraid that their faith had been undermined.

Today the fragment has been translated and is found in at least three collections of translations of the Dead Sea Scrolls. First to appear was R. Eisenman and M. Wise's *The Dead Sea Scrolls Uncovered.* In it the controversial text is translated as follows:

> They will enter into Judgement with . . . (4) and they will put to death the Leader of the Community, the Bran[ch of David] (this might also be read, depending on the context, "and the Leader of the Community, the Bran[ch of David]," will put him to death).[1]

It was good that they provided the second option, and while their first choice is conceivable it is not probable. Both G. Vermes in *The Dead Sea Scrolls in English* and F. García Martínez in *The Dead Sea Scrolls Translated* correctly translate the Hebrew verb (*whmytw*) "will kill him."[2] The fragment is not sensational, therefore, and is like so many other Jewish writings before the defeat of the messianic figure Simon Bar Cochba in 135 C.E. That is, the Qumran fragment refers not to the killing of the messiah, which would align this text with earliest Christian proclamations. It refers, rather, to a messiah who shall kill Israel's enemies.[3] The fragment is hardly, as an author claims, "potentially very explosive."[4] As O. Betz and R. Riesner point out, to interpret this Qumran text to refer to the death of a messiah "is fundamentally untenable."[5] Thus, rather than revealing a set pre-Christian Jewish concept into which Christian proclamation about Jesus neatly fits, the Qumran fragment indicates a fundamental difference between the Essenes and the earliest followers of Jesus. Only the latter attributed their concept of salvation to the actions of one messianic figure named

Jesus. As E. Käsemann stated in *Jesus Means Freedom,* "Our faith
rests on what Adolf Schlatter, in his last little book, expressed
in the question: 'Do we know Jesus?,' and on nothing else,
whatever the volumes of dogmatics and creeds may consider
necessary."[6]

This one controversial episode focused on the sensational
nature of the Dead Sea Scrolls. It highlights for me the necessity
of addressing to a wide audience some reflections, certainly my
own, on the Dead Sea Scrolls. There are claims that the Vatican has been hiding some of the Dead Sea Scrolls because they
allegedly contain ideas that would tend to falsify the claims of
Christians. What are the Dead Sea Scrolls? Are they a hindrance
or a boon for Christians, or does the answer lie somewhere in
between?

DEAD SEA SCROLLS: DEFINITIONS

At the outset it is best to define our major terms. Much con-
fusion has been caused by misconceptions and the use of
language that means one thing to the speaker but another to
the audience. First and foremost, the Dead Sea Scrolls were
not found in the Dead Sea, despite the fact that the Library
of Congress placarded its feature on them with the words
"Scrolls from the Dead Sea."[7] Journalists constantly misunder-
stand them and highlight new discoveries with titles such as
"Sea scrolls mystery may get new chapter."[8] The Dead Sea
Scrolls have nothing to do with the sea — let alone the Dead
Sea. If these leather and papyrus scrolls had been cast into the
Dead Sea they would not have lasted a day, let alone two thousand years. In the spring of 68 C.E. precious documents were
hidden by the Qumran Essenes in caves that are located just
to the west of the Dead Sea. They hid them either expecting
to return and continue their study of them, or perhaps to take
them to Jerusalem so as to celebrate with the Messiah in the
New Jerusalem. They never returned. Many Essenes, as Jose-

phus reports, were killed by the Romans, others probably died in the subsequent famine in Jerusalem. Some probably died on Masada, since Essene documents were discovered on this desert fortress.

At least some escaped and most likely joined other communities — in my judgment the Jewish communities that have shaped for us the Gospels of Matthew and John.[9] What was found by a Bedouin in late 1947, just before the establishment of Israel, was the remains of a Jewish library that dates from the time of Jesus. The library belonged to the Essenes, especially those living at Qumran. They were the strict branch of the Essene sect. Far fewer than 170 Essenes lived at Qumran, to judge by the size of the general room in which they ate and worshipped. Most Essenes lived throughout ancient Palestine.[10] According to Philo and Josephus they consisted of more than four thousand devout Jews who lived throughout ancient Palestine.[11]

WHAT WAS FOUND IN THE LIBRARY?

Eleven caves held approximately six hundred writings. Many of these writings were completely unknown to scholars. They were never cited in ancient documents, so there was no reason to imagine they existed. Twelve of these scrolls contained copies of the *Rule of the Community*,[12] a collection of the rules of the Qumran Community which ends with a psalm. One of the first scholars to work on it — Millar Burrows — said it reminded him of the *Methodist Book of Discipline*, and so for decades it was called the *Manual of Discipline*.

One scroll contained a copy of the hymnbook of the Community. Because it is characterized by psalms of thanksgiving, it is named the *Thanksgiving Hymns*. Another scroll contained a description of the final war between the forces of light and the forces of darkness; it is called the *War Scroll*. Yet another significant scroll contained the Qumranites' commentary on the book

of Habakkuk. In it we learn that God did not disclose to Habakkuk the meaning of his words. Indeed, all the mysteries of the
words of God's servants, the prophets, were disclosed only to
the Righteous Teacher (1QpHab 7).

Who is this mysterious and anonymous teacher always
referred to obliquely as the Righteous Teacher? Despite impres-
sive and erudite attempts by scholars, we cannot identify him
with any person known from history or ancient documents. He
was surely the priest who led a group from the Jerusalem Temple into the wilderness and to Qumran around 150 B.C.E. He
may not have been the founder of the sect, but he was the one
who founded the Community at Qumran, on the western shores
of the Dead Sea. He must have been a brilliant and charismatic
leader, and if portions of the *Thanksgiving Hymns* were composed by him, then he felt he was chosen by God to establish
the eternal planting for God's glory.[13]

What else was found in the library? In addition to the un-
known writings, many books of the so-called Apocrypha and
Pseudepigrapha were found. Every book of the Old Testament
(= Hebrew Bible) was recovered, except perhaps Esther. This
ancient Jewish library thus contained writings inherited by the
Qumran Essenes, as well as those they composed.[14]

It is the previously unknown documents that have in-
trigued so many throughout the world. Many feel that out of the
desert caves come insights and information that might falsify,
or at least undermine, Christian dogma and doctrine. Before
we delve into such issues, it is best to ascertain what is meant
by "Christianity" and "Christian faith." Many television evangelists have confused the masses about what is important for
Christians. Obviously a definition of these key terms which derives from a sociological analysis of contemporary phenomena
will be useless and misleading in discerning how and what
ways, if at all, the Dead Sea Scrolls might be important for
Christians.

WHAT IS CHRISTIAN FAITH?

A warning can be learned by studying the noun "faith" and the verb "to believe" in the New Testament. In the words of Jesus and in Paul's epistles "faith" has primarily a verbal and dynamic function. To believe is what someone does. That is, it is an act, a commitment to Jesus and for what he stands. In the Gospel of John "faith" as a noun never appears, but the author uses the verb "to believe" or "to have faith" more than any other evangelist.[15] Thus, the Fourth Evangelist is careful to distance himself from those who think "faith" can be considered a static and set category. The Fourth Evangelist states explicitly that he has written his work so that the reader "may believe," that is, perform an act — do something. In the later writings of the New Testament this brilliant theological insight is missed. In fact, one author — the author of Titus, whether Paul, or more likely, a follower of Paul — can even urge his readers to be sound in the faith (Titus 1:13, cf. 2:2), indicating that the noun "faith" had drained the verb "to have faith" of its living nature and dynamic quality.

Christianity thus begins with an individual's personal commitment to Jesus. What must one believe? Many Christians demand so much in answering this question that once again the verb is lost and the noun dominates. Rather than life and freedom, as Käsemann perceived, the death of what Jesus and his earliest followers inaugurated becomes manifest. The Christian is freed, as Paul stresses in Galatians 5; yet virtually everywhere are those who want to entrap and enslave people into believing what obviously tends to involve absurdities. At the heart of Christian belief is the conviction that God was in Christ Jesus. That means that Jesus is the Way to God, as brilliantly explained both in the Gospel of John and in Hebrews.

While we now have over a dozen gospels from the first three centuries of Christianity and hundreds of writings claiming to be sacred scripture, or considered such by many Jewish contemporaries of Jesus, the Christian does not have to study them to learn what is essential to believe in Jesus. As the Protestant Reformers stressed, and most Roman Catholics now agree, Jesus' life and message as recorded in the Bible provide us with all that is necessary for salvation (*sola scriptura*). That is to say, no one has received authority from God to damn you if you do not believe that Jesus was born of a virgin, walked on water, and turned water into wine.

Christian faith is not a commitment to concepts or even aspects of Jesus' life. It is a personal commitment to God in the sense that this belief is centered in how God was manifest in one particular person, Jesus of Nazareth. It is important to note that Paul constantly urged his reader to believe in Jesus, but never reduced the content of that belief to a series of nouns or concepts. Moreover, when he compared the importance of faith, hope, and love, he unequivocally opted for love: "and the greatest of these is love" (1 Cor. 13:13). I see this as a warning: we must not define the content of faith for another Christian and thereby erode the living love that defines the Christian (John 13:34).

WHAT ABOUT CHRISTIAN DOGMA?

Obviously, rigid dogmas may well be shattered by historical discoveries. Christian faith that has succumbed to rigor mortis needs to be recognized as such and buried. That is not to jettison all creeds, for surely some creed is necessary for each Christian. But a creed does not have to be written in ancient dogmatics, and this freedom has given rise to some attractive creeds and confessions written during the twentieth century.[16]

Dogmatics has been important in Christian history to clarify and defend the faith. That should be acknowledged, but it does not mean that what was defined as Christian faith for St. Augustine must be operative and constricting for us today. I am convinced that Augustine would have been opposed to such a move. It is now clear that we have insights into Jesus' time which Augustine did not know about, and that this new information, as well as the cultural climate at the end of the second millennium, necessitates finding new ways of expressing our understanding of Christian faith. Augustine struggled to shape faith — rather, the art of believing — for his time. Do we not have the same responsibility?

If so, we should not begin our inquiry by defining Christian dogmatics and seeking to discern how, if at all, the ideas and perceptions in the Dead Sea Scrolls are synonymous or challenge set dogmas. Ironically, the Dead Sea Scrolls are much older than Christian dogmatics, but they are new to us — and they often, in my experience, are more sensitive to the ways God has been attempting to reach us. We New Testament experts initially must not worry how, if at all, our work impinges upon that of the theologians and dogmaticians. We must keep focused on our essential task: understanding the documents within the New Testament in their own time and setting first, and then seeking to express, as Christians, how they impact our task of being faithful to our Creator in the present and in the future. The two tasks must be understood to be conceptually and methodologically separate, even if there is a circuitous flow in the dialectic of seeking to understand them back then and us today and tomorrow.

FEAR

Why have some Christians been alarmed by, and even afraid of, the Dead Sea Scrolls? Why do they fear these Jewish writings may disprove the teachings and creeds of the church?

Individuals who raise such questions usually are impressed by three points, which may be summarized as follows: First, they are concerned that the Dead Sea Scrolls, which were discovered in the winter of 1947, were distributed only to Christians, mostly Roman Catholics, for publication. Second, they have been told, and believe, that now, fifty years later, most of the Dead Sea Scrolls have not been published. Finally, they ask a logical question: Have Christian scholars seen something in the scrolls that may prove destructive, or embarrassing, to Christian beliefs?

Some people, a little more informed, ask why the scrolls have shattered the faith of two members of the original team of editors, an Englishman and a French scholar. What is in the scrolls that would cause John M. Allegro to turn vehemently anti-Christian? In the 1950s Allegro wrote John Strugnell, "I shouldn't worry about that theological job if I were you. By the time I'm finished there won't be any church left for you to join."[17] What led Père Joazef Tadeusz Milik, a Polish Roman Catholic and one of the greatest experts on the Qumran fragments, to leave the priesthood?

When informed of these events some people surmise that there is a Vatican conspiracy to hide from the public these documents written near Jesus' time. I intend to struggle with such questions honestly. Unenlightened Christians may be surprised by what I have to say.

The readers need to be informed that seven scrolls were found in Cave 1. Three of them were obtained by one of the leading scholars in the Hebrew University in Jerusalem, Elazar L. Sukenik. These three are the *War Scroll,* the *Thanksgiving Hymns,* and the *Isaiah Scroll.* The other four scrolls were brought to the United States by the Syrian metropolitan of Jerusalem, Mar Athanasius Y. Samuel, who advertised them for sale in the *Wall Street Journal.* Surprisingly, Yigael Yadin, Sukenik's son, was able to purchase them and thus the other four scrolls were taken back to the Near East, this time to what was then the western side of Jerusalem. The four are the *Great Isaiah Scroll,* the *Rule of the Community* (1QS), the *Genesis Apocryphon* (1QapGen), and the *Habakkuk Pesher* (1QpHab). Thus, all seven of the large scrolls found in Cave 1 eventually ended up in the Shrine of the Book in Jerusalem.

In that famous city, revered as the Holy City by Jews, Christians, and Muslims, the seven scrolls were studied and edited by Jewish scholars living in Jerusalem. The first was Sukenik, followed by his son Yadin, who took a Jewish name, following the custom of many Israelis. The first critical editions of both the *Rule of the Community* and the *Thanksgiving Hymns* were by Jacob Licht, a Jew living in Jerusalem. Thus, it is incorrect to state that the Dead Sea Scrolls were published only by Christians.

Jewish scholars, as well as Christians, refer to the Qumran Community as a monastery, conclude that the Jews living at Qumran were a strict branch of the Essenes, and stress the paradigmatic importance of the Dead Sea Scrolls for an improved understanding of Jesus and the origins of Christianity. Such conclusions have been obvious in the major books published by David Flusser, an Israeli, and Geza Vermes, a Hungarian Jew who has recently retired from teaching in Oxford University. Most attractive are Flusser's *Judaism and the Origins of Christianity,*[18] and his popular *The Spiritual History of the Dead Sea Sect,* and Vermes's *The Dead Sea Scrolls: Qumran in Perspective.*[19]

Was Jesus really influenced by others, including his contemporaries? In light of the creative ideas found in the Dead Sea Scrolls, some Christians are afraid that they no longer can look up to and idolize Jesus. They think that Jesus taught a concept of God which was unique to him, and that it was revealed only to him. Now, seeing some ideas considered unique to Jesus appearing in the Dead Sea Scrolls seems to disturb some Christians; among such ideas are the concept of the Holy Spirit, and the references to God's kingdom. Jesus quoted Isaiah and others. He spoke Aramaic, the language of his people, the Jews. In order to communicate he needed to speak to them in their own terms, concepts, and perspectives. Unlike other Jewish teachers, like Hillel, Shammai, Gamaliel, and Johanan ben Zakkai, he did not base his thought on that of others. He was saluted for his authoritative pronouncements.

If Jesus quoted others, does that not make him inferior to them? The best minds are inspired by other great minds. Those inspired are also inspired by others who have received God's word. For example, Jesus inspired both Mahatma Gandhi and Martin Luther King Jr. But, one might reply, Jesus was not a mere man like Gandhi and King. Christians must grant that point, but that does not mean Jesus was not influenced by others. The creeds do not stress that he was God; they clarify that Jesus was fully human and fully divine. The former demands that he was a man of his time and influenced by others. Does the New Testament not make it obvious that Jesus was influenced by the Syrophenician woman and the Roman centurion? If so, would it have been even more obvious that he was influenced by fellow devout Jews?

Are the Dead Sea Scrolls dangerous for Christians? Did not some of the early editors of the Dead Sea Scrolls become atheists, and does that not prove that the scrolls are dangerous for Christians? While it is clear that Milik left the priesthood, it certainly does not follow that he is no longer a believer in the traditional sense. My conversations with him in August 1996 convinced me of a warm, brilliant mind, and a scholar who has deep Christian convictions.

Is it not clear, others might argue, that John Allegro certainly could not be considered a Christian? Certainly he was not a Christian when he died, even though he was a Methodist when he began his academic career. I wonder, however, just how Christian was he before he began to edit the scrolls? We do not know how rigid and dogmatic, even blind, was his commitment to Christianity. From reading his numerous books, I see nothing in them from the Dead Sea Scrolls that changed his faith. Most of his interpretations are idiosyncratic and often absurd. Perhaps the discovery of sensationally important manuscripts brought out the sinister side of Allegro. The fault would then not lie in the Dead Sea Scrolls but in his own soul.

There is no reason to be concerned about any threat from the Dead Sea Scrolls. Most editors who were Christians remain faithful after studying and editing the scrolls. Many become even more committed to Christianity. Obviously, their own faith has developed and matured. Among these are the former bishop of Stockholm and dean of Harvard Divinity School Krister Stendahl. I should also mention Father Joseph Fitzmyer, Father Ray Brown, Father Roland Murphy, Eugene Ulrich, John Collins, Jerome Murphy-O'Connor, Carol Newsom, Jim Roberts, Eileen Schuller, Emile Puech, Adela Yarbro Collins, James VanderKam, Stephen Pfann, Craig Evans, Martin Hengel, Hermann Lichtenberger, James Sanders, Frank Cross, and many others.

What could be found in a Jewish library from Jesus' time that could tarnish or disprove the faith of a Christian today? Would the recovery of Jesus' marriage license even disturb some Christians? That conceptual possibility is virtually unthinkable. I cannot imagine anything in the Qumran library that would hinder Christian faith; of course, I am referring to informed Christian faith, which grows and changes as it is more enlightened. My own faith is considerably different from the one I held when I entered Duke Divinity School. And I hope that my faith will change and grow even more in the next decades, if I should be so lucky. That is not to suggest that the message of Jesus has changed. As Paul Tillich stated, "'Kerygmatic' theology is related to fundamentalism and orthodoxy in so far as it emphasizes the unchangeable truth of the message (kerygma) over against the changing demands of the situation."[20]

HOW THEN ARE THE SCROLLS IMPORTANT TO CHRISTIANS, ESPECIALLY IF THEY DO NOT MENTION JESUS?

It is imperative to clarify that the Dead Sea Scrolls never mention Jesus. They also never refer in any way to the apostles. The scrolls are documents actually held by Jesus' contemporaries and his fellow Jews. Jesus shared with the Qumran Essenes the teaching about God's kingdom (see *Angelic Liturgy*), the dream of a better world, and the literary form of the beatitudes (see

4Q525; *Beatitudes*) He was antithetical to the Essenes in his teaching on the Sabbath and his unique perception of love, as I have tried to demonstrate in *Jesus and the Dead Sea Scrolls.*[21]

Having studied the scrolls since 1957, what have I learned about Christian faith? Christian faith is vibrant and alive; we are freed by Christ for freedom (Gal. 5:1). We do not need the rules and regulations of Qumran, nor do we need to pass a final examination after more than two years of scrutiny before we are admitted to Jesus' community. While the Qumranites had such barriers, Jesus simply called and Jews followed him. Of course, like the Qumranites he demanded leaving all, especially wealth, behind, and making a full unequivocal commitment to God and his Kingdom. From the Qumranites we should learn not only to believe that God is present when we pray, but to move on to experience the presence of our Creator in praying, as did the Qumranites.

Listening to the authors of the Dead Sea Scrolls, feeling their attractive oneness, and admiring their utter dedication to God through a life lived out on a marl terrace or in caves just to the west of the foul-smelling Dead Sea, invokes in me the importance of the social world in which we live. Jesus did not live in the desert or in the wilderness. He left the wilderness and lived and taught in the villages and in the fields where the average person toiled. Thus, I agree with W. Pannenberg that "while the identity of individuals is indeed mediated through the social context of their lives, nonetheless it has its root and ground only in their relation to God."[22] I might have said "primarily" and not "only."

Has my faith been strengthened by studying the scrolls for nearly forty years? Absolutely! Now I can imagine life in Bethsaida, Capernaum, Jerusalem, Gamla, and at Qumran in the first century when Jesus was alive. That is because I have spent time walking through the first-century streets or passageways of these places, seeing the objects held by his contemporaries, feeling the topography that he also experienced, and sitting for hours in one of the Qumran caves or *feeling the ruins* the Qumran

Essenes left behind. The scrolls contain ideas that help me understand both the origin of my faith and the living of it in the end of the second millennium. For example, from the scrolls I have obtained profound insights into the meaning of some ideas (like the origin of evil and strict monotheism), metaphors (like "living water," "the eternal planting"), concepts (like "heaven," "community," the end-time), terms (like Messiah and Kingdom [especially of God]), and particularly the importance of cherishing difficult dreams (a better age when evil will disappear).

For example, from the *War Scroll* I learn how powerful evil may become and often is: not even the archangels and all the hosts of heaven, fighting alongside the Qumranites, can defeat Satan and his legions. Only God can, and he does so immediately once he enters the final battle. That means the end of time will be even better than the beginning of it. Humans will be one with nature, with each other, and with themselves, and especially with God in an Eden-like setting that will not have the potential of disobedience. The Righteous Teacher of Qumran was convinced he was planting the trees for the eternal planting, that is, his faithful followers.

Surely the eschatological nature of the teachings found in the Dead Sea Scrolls, in Jesus' authentic sayings, and in Paul's letters helps us agree with J. Moltmann that their God is "the God whom we therefore cannot really have in us or over us but always only before us, who encounters us in his promises for the future, and whom we therefore cannot 'have' either, but can only await in active hope."[23] The scrolls help us understand that the God we have known in tradition, in scripture, and in our own lives is indeed the one who has gone on before us.

I must confess I have often been disturbed and embarrassed by what I see the institution called "the church" doing. But for me there is a vast difference between the church I love and the institution that is necessary. As Hans Küng in *On Being A Christian* states, "The Church is not the kingdom of God, but it is — or should be — *spokesman and witness* for the kingdom of God."[24]

CONCLUSION

The Dead Sea Scrolls have revolutionized our understanding of Christian origins. From them we have learned concepts and terms we did not know had appeared within Jewish theology. We appreciate the genius and creativity of Jesus' Jewish contemporaries. The scrolls help us reconstruct and appreciate the world in which Jesus lived and from which Christianity evolved. Most important, they awaken us to the task of striving to understand Jesus' message and life, and the claims of the first Christians within the milieu that gave birth to Christianity. Christians should be proud of their inheritance.

NOTES

1. R. Eisenman and M. Wise, *The Dead Sea Scrolls Uncovered* (Rockport, Mass.: Element, 1992), 29.

2. G. Vermes, *The Dead Sea Scrolls in English*, 4th ed. (New York: Penguin Books, 1995), 150; F. García Martínez, *The Dead Sea Scrolls Translated: The Qumran Texts in English*, trans. W. G. E. Watson, 2nd ed. (Grand Rapids: Eerdmans, 1996), 124.

3. For a classic reference to this idea, which dates from the latter part of the first century B.C.E., see the *Psalms of Solomon* 17 and 18.

4. Eisenman and Wise, *Dead Sea Scrolls Uncovered*, 24.

5. O. Betz and R. Riesner, *Jesus, Qumran, and the Vatican: Clarifications* (New York: Crossroad, 1994), 86.

6. E. Käsemann, *Jesus Means Freedom*, trans. F. Clarke (Philadelphia: Fortress, 1970), 21.

7. A. Sussmann and R. Peled, eds., *Scrolls from the Dead Sea* (Washington, D.C.: Library of Congress, 1993).

8. Associated Press, Tuesday, December 19, 1995.

9. See especially, K. Stendahl, *The School of St. Matthew* (1954; Philadelphia: Fortress, 1968 [with a new introduction]); Charlesworth, ed., *John and the Dead Sea Scrolls* (New York: Crossroad, 1991).

10. For a succinct and popular account of the discovery of the DSS and their importance, see Charlesworth, "Introduction and History," in *The Dead Sea Scrolls: Rule of the Community; Photographic Multi-Language Edition*, ed. Charlesworth et al. (New York: Continuum, 1996), 11–30.

11. For a reliable summary on the Essenes see J. J. Collins, "Essenes," in *ABD* 2:619–26.

12. For critical texts and translations, see Charlesworth et al., eds., *Rule of the Community and Related Documents,* Princeton Theological Seminary Dead Sea Scrolls Project 1 (Louisville: Westminster/John Knox Press, 1994).

13. See Charlesworth, "The Righteous Teacher and the Historical Jesus," in *Earthing Christologies,* ed. Charlesworth and W. P. Weaver, Faith and Scholarship Colloquies (Valley Forge: Trinity Press International, 1995), 46–61.

14. For lists and categories see Charlesworth in *Dead Sea Scrolls,* 11–30.

15. The Greek verb *pisteúein* occurs 11 times in Matthew, 14 in Mark, 9 in Luke, and 98 in John. It also appears 54 times in the letters attributed to Paul.

16. I especially like the Korean Creed and the Creed of 1967.

17. See his letter of December 1955, quoted by M. Baigent and R. Leigh, *The Dead Sea Scrolls Deception* (New York: Summit Books, 1991), 46.

18. David Flusser, *Judaism and the Origins of Christianity,* ed. B. Young (Jerusalem: Magnes Press, 1988). See Charlesworth, "David Flusser's Vision," in *Explorations* 4.1 (1990): 1, 4.

19. David Flusser, *The Spiritual History of the Dead Sea Sect,* trans. C. Glucker (Tel-Aviv: MOD Books, 1989); Geza Vermes, *The Dead Sea Scrolls: Qumran in Perspective* (Cleveland: Collins, 1978).

20. P. Tillich, *Systematic Theology* (Chicago: University of Chicago Press, 1951), 1:4.

21. Charlesworth, *Jesus and the Dead Sea Scrolls,* AB Reference Library (New York: Doubleday, 1992, 1995).

22. W. Pannenberg, *Anthropology in Theological Perspective,* trans. M. J. O'Connell (Philadelphia: Westminster, 1985), 480.

23. J. Moltmann, *Theology of Hope,* trans. J. W. Leitch (London: SCM, 1967), 16.

24. H. Küng, *On Being a Christian,* trans. E. Quinn (Garden City, N.Y.: Doubleday, 1984), 504 (italics his).

Index of Subjects and Authors